MURDER
IN VICTORIAN
SCOTLAND

Emile L'Angelier

Madeleine Smith

MURDER
IN VICTORIAN SCOTLAND

The Trial of Madeleine Smith

Douglas MacGowan

For Uncle Wally & Aunt Max —
Love,

Doug MacG.

PRAEGER

Westport, Connecticut
London

Library of Congress Cataloging-in-Publication Data

MacGowan, Douglas, 1963–
    Murder in Victorian Scotland : the trial of Madeleine Smith /
Douglas MacGowan.
      p.   cm.
    Includes bibliographical references and index.
    ISBN 0–275–96431–0 (alk. paper)
    1. Smith, Madeleine Hamilton, 1835–1928. 2. Murder—Scotland—
History—19th century. 3. Trials (Murder)—Scotland—History—19th
century. 4. Poisoning—Scotland—Case studies. I. Title.
HV6535.G5S35   1999
364.15'23'0941443—dc21   99–13792

British Library Cataloguing in Publication Data is available.

Library of Congress Catalog Card Number: 99–13792
ISBN: 0–275–96431–0

First published in 1999

Praeger Publishers, 88 Post Road West, Westport, CT 06881
An imprint of Greenwood Publishing Group, Inc.
www.praeger.com

Printed in the United States of America

The paper used in this book complies with the
Permanent Paper Standard issued by the National
Information Standards Organization (Z39.48–1984).

10 9 8 7 6 5 4 3 2 1

Contents

Acknowledgments

I would like to thank the following persons who provided me with information or resources, without which I could not have completed this book: Clare Connelly for insight into the ramifications of Madeleine Smith's trial; Carol Docherty and Ian Wright for the tour of the Blythswood Square house; Peter Duff for information on the current status of the *not proven* verdict; John Lauper for the census information; Kay Munro for the nineteenth-century maps of Glasgow; Sally Raeside for the newspaper articles; Heather Staines, for all the help along the way; Louis Stott for information on the movie *Madeleine* and the Smith's home at Rhu; my parents and family for their encouragement and support; and J. Christopher Weiman for the illustrations.

And special thanks to my wife, April, my other femme fatale.

Introduction

Not proven is unique to Scotland; juries sitting for criminal trials there have three options when returning a verdict: *guilty*, *not guilty*, and *not proven*. Both the *not guilty* and *not proven* verdicts allow the defendant to go free. The *not proven* verdict often carries a stigma, however, as it not only indicates that the prosecution failed to prove its case, but also states that the defense failed to convince the jury of the defendant's innocence.

Debate on retaining the "Scottish verdict," which has fluctuated over the years, reached a pinnacle in 1992, when family members of homicide victims, outraged at seeing the accused murderers freed due to inadequate prosecution evidence, circulated petitions to eliminate the verdict from the Scottish legal system. Polls conducted at the time showed that jurors were only rarely instructed on the precise differences between a *not guilty* and a *not proven* verdict, and that almost 50 percent of Scots did not understand the legal implications or basis of the *not proven* verdict.

The verdict remains valid, despite the 1992 protests, although debate on the three-verdict system will undoubtedly continue.

Madeleine Smith was not the first defendant to receive a *not proven* judgment, nor would she be the last. But she stands as one of the earliest and strongest examples of an accused murderer whose celebrity extended long past the trial.

Part I

March 23, 1857

IN THE MIDDLE OF A DREAM, THE BELLS BEGAN.

The clamor of the doorbells jolted Mrs. Ann Jenkins from the soft comfort of sleep to the darkness of her room and the violent commotion at the front door of her Glasgow lodging house.

The clock in the hall struck half past two.

Opening the door, Mrs. Jenkins found Emile L'Angelier, one of her lodgers, doubled over and gripping his stomach. "I am very bad," he whispered, reaching up toward her. "I am going to have another vomiting of that bile." Mrs. Jenkins helped him into the small room he rented and asked if he had taken medicine or any food that might have made him sick. He said he had not.

Emile's condition continued to deteriorate, and five o'clock saw Mrs. Jenkins going through the early dawn of Glasgow to the house of Dr. James Steven on Stafford Place. Dr. Steven, ill himself, told Mrs. Jenkins to give her tenant hot water with drops of laudanum, to put a mustard poultice on his stomach, and to come back later in the morning if the man did not improve.

When she returned, Emile told her he had never been able to tolerate laudanum and he also refused the mustard plaster. Sipping a few mouthfuls of hot water instead, he instantly vomited a foul-smelling liquid into a nearby chamber pot.

Several blocks away, in the house of architect James Smith, the servants of the household awoke at 6:30 and began their first chores. As usual, most of the Smith family would breakfast in bed, and gather later in the dining room or sitting room to formally begin their day.

If anyone noticed something amiss with the eldest daughter of the Smith family on that cold morning, nobody spoke of it. She had been out of sorts for quite some time and was most likely preoccupied with the planning of her upcoming wedding.

By seven o'clock, Emile had taken a further turn for the worse, and Mrs. Jenkins went out again and brought Dr. Steven back to her lodging house. The physician looked into Emile's eyes, felt tenderly around his stomach, applied a mustard poultice, and then left, promising to return between ten and eleven that morning.

At nine o'clock, Emile asked Mrs. Jenkins to send for his friend, Miss Mary Perry. Mrs. Jenkins's son was sent to fetch her.

Dr. Steven returned as promised, and Mrs. Jenkins waited in the hallway as the physician went in to check on his patient. Dr. Steven felt for a pulse, then lifted Emile's head and let it drop back onto the pillow. "Draw the rest of these curtains," he said softly. "The man is dead."

The drawing of the curtains in Emile's small room started a web that spun quickly outward and would, in the space of one week, lead to the discovery of stacks of illicit love letters, cause someone intimately close to the deceased to flee Glasgow, and see James Smith's eldest daughter, Madeleine, arrested for the murder of her lover, Emile L'Angelier.

Part II

Prelude

THE CHANNEL ISLANDS, nestled between France and England in the English Channel, have been populated since prehistoric times, as Paleolithic remains attest. The largest of the islands is Jersey, known to the conquering Romans as *Ceasarea*, named after their emperor. The island features a majestic patchwork landscape of steep cliffs and dark caves, sandy beaches and deep valleys. During the Norman Conquest of 1066, the island officially fell under English rule, although its culture and language would continue to be a fluctuating mixture of English and French, as waves of people from both countries came to the island to avoid political oppression or to start life anew.

Pierre Jean Langelier was one of the swarm, leaving his native France to avoid political persecution. Decidedly anti-monarchist, he and his brother left the France ruled by Louis XVIII in 1813 and settled on Jersey. They fit in well with the natives and other immigrants, and the siblings quickly established a relatively successful business as nurserymen.

Their small shop was located near the family of Claude Marie de la Croix, a wealthy merchant by Jersey standards. Young Pierre became attracted to Claude's eldest daughter, Victoire Melanie, and he pursued her for months according to the customs and social manners of the time. If Mr. de la Croix had any reservations about Victoire's fortuneless suitor, he was eventually won over. He blessed the union, and Pierre and Victoire were married in July of 1822 at the Chapel of St. Louis in St. Helier.

The young couple set up shop as seed merchants, hoping to attract the business of the British gentry who were eager to grow unusual flowers and lush fruit trees on their Jersey estates or in their manor gardens back home.

On the last day of April 1823, almost nine months to the day from their wedding, Pierre and Victoire welcomed their first child, Pierre Emile Langelier, who would always be known as Emile. The family expanded the following year with a daughter, Anastasie Melanie, and increased further over the next ten years with two more daughters and another son, Achille.

The Langelier family lived in the same small building that housed their shop, as was the custom—but as the family grew, the need for a larger house became inevitable. After investigating several possible locations, Pierre moved his family to a shop near La Place Royale, which housed Jersey's government offices. Pierre hoped to attract the foot traffic of the wealthy visitors and government officials who hurried in and out of La Place at all hours.

Young Emile lived the life of an ordinary Jersey boy in the early nineteenth century: he played with friends in the narrow streets, watched over his younger siblings, and listened to the stories his parents told of France. He attended classes at the National School and learned English, a language he picked up quickly and soon spoke almost as well as he did the French of his household.

When he reached a responsible age, Emile was allowed to help his parents in the seed shop, as it was assumed that he would one day take over the family business. But Pierre hoped to see the business grow beyond the mere selling of seeds, and sought to train Emile in all aspects of the nursery business beyond the realm of a seed shop. Ironically, the logical step was to have the young boy serve an apprenticeship with a competitor, an Englishman named Saunders who had a large nursery near the Langelier home. Saunders's business was more modern and catered to the British, a clientele that Pierre greatly wanted to attract. The Langeliers met with Saunders to hammer out the details of a contract, and, after reaching a mutually satisfactory agreement, Emile began a five-year apprenticeship in Saunders's shop.

Initially, Emile felt like he had landed on another planet. Working daily among the English-speaking people, he learned of British culture, of Europe, and of a life very different from all he had ever known. The idea of living somewhere else began to grow more and more appealing to his young mind.

The apprenticeship proved successful for everyone, and Emile grew into a handsome and hard-working young man. His family's shop continued to do a good business, and all things were pointing toward a bright future. Unexpectedly, however, Pierre became ill and died in 1840. Victoire was terrified, unprepared for the demands of a widow's life with five young children and a demanding business. Legally, Emile inherited the seed shop, but he was still in the midst of his apprenticeship, and did not want to eliminate his mother's sole source of income. When the family gathered after Pierre's burial to discuss their various options, it was decided that Emile should continue his apprenticeship, and Victoire and sixteen-year-old Anastasie would continue with the daily chores of running the seed shop.

In 1842, as Emile was nearing the end of his apprenticeship, a wealthy gentleman paid several visits to Saunders's nursery. Sir Francis Mackenzie of Gairloch owned vast lands in the Rosshire area of Scotland, and took an instant liking to the hard-working Emile. Mackenzie soon proposed taking the seventeen-year-old back with him to work on his Conanbridge estate near Cromarty Firth.

Saunders believed that Sir Francis would provide a better opportunity for Emile's growth, so he agreed to an early release from the apprenticeship. Victoire, after being promised that Emile would earn a good wage and send some of that money home to Jersey, consented.

With a mixture of excitement and loss, the Langelier family followed Emile down to the small harbor and watched him board the boat that would take him to Southampton, where he would catch a train north to Scotland, as foreign and unknown a place to the Langeliers as the Antarctic.

Rather than going immediately to Conanbridge, Sir Francis sent Emile for training at Dicksons and Company, an Edinburgh nursery with whom he had done a great deal of business. Once Emile received a complete education in the plants he was likely to encounter on Sir Francis's lands, he would go to the Conanbridge estate.

Again, Emile's future looked bright. After some initial homesickness and culture shock, the young man settled readily into the busy capital of Scotland, and he impressed the customers and management of Dicksons with his hard work and intelligence.

In June of 1843, after Emile had learned much and was mentally preparing for his move to Conanbridge, Sir Francis had a stroke and died. Emile was suddenly on the edge of destitution, with neither the funds to return to Jersey nor enough to continue living in Edinburgh if he found himself unemployed. His sole hope was to remain with Dicksons and Company, although his placement in the firm was completely dependent on a now nonbinding agreement with the deceased Sir Francis. He sent a hasty letter to his mother, expressing anxiety about his future.

Frantic, he met with William Richardson, a senior member in the Dicksons administration, and said he hoped to retain his position in the company. Richardson expressed complete satisfaction with Emile's work and said he saw no problem in keeping him on. Emile was overjoyed and wrote another hurried letter to his mother, telling her that all was well.

At some point during his few hours of free time in Edinburgh, Emile became acquainted with a young lady with whom he became deeply enamored, and the two may have been engaged. This "young lady from Fife" would resurface again after Emile's death, although her identity has never been revealed.

The years wore on and Emile's homesickness returned. He grew tired of the persistent gray weather of Edinburgh, and his relationship with the young lady from Fife turned somewhat colder. He saved his wages and journeyed back to Jersey in 1846, staying with his mother and siblings.

Almost immediately, however, he realized his mistake. He had grown homesick for Jersey while he was away from it, but the slow pace of the island was far too monotonous and confining after the noise and bustle of Edinburgh. He told his family he needed to leave home again. The family gathered for open discussion, as they always did for such important decisions, and it was eventually decided that Emile should go to France and stay with his mother's relatives.

He landed a job as a clerk for a Paris merchant, and his good looks and charming manner came into their full fruition. He spent little time with his mother's family, concentrating instead on the late nights and easy pleasures of the French capital. He courted young ladies, obsessively pursuing them and then affecting near suicidal frenzies when one of them decided to leave him. Almost creating a new identity for himself, he shed his skin as a working-class nurseryman and became one of the army of young men who haunted the night entertainments of the city, discussing philosophy and the tragedy of lost loves. To complete his transformation, he changed the spelling of his surname from *Langelier* to *L'Angelier*, the authentic French spelling that his ancestors had used before his father's flight from France thirty years earlier.

Believing that the military might enhance the glamorous image he was actively cultivating, Emile volunteered for service during the Revolution of 1848, but spent less than a month serving as a guard at a railway station outside Paris. Initially disappointed at the lack of combat, he would later inflate his small experience into gallant stories of his service during the Revolution.

Emile probably would have continued in this carefree lifestyle had not a summons come from Jersey in 1851. His little sister, Zephirine, the second to youngest, had died. The girl had always been sickly and required a lot of care. Consequently, she had been the favorite of Victoire, who grieved terribly over the loss. The young girl was buried next to her father, and life attempted to return to normal in the family seed shop.

After comforting his mother as best he could, Emile's metropolitan soul once again grew restless with the sluggish life of Jersey—but instead of journeying back to France, he decided to return to Scotland. Why he made this choice remains a puzzle, as he did not have particularly fond memories of his time in Edinburgh, but perhaps he felt himself a new person after his five years in Paris and wanted to conquer Scotland anew. He may also have wanted to rekindle the relationship with the young woman in Fife.

He arrived in Edinburgh and tried once again to obtain a job at Dicksons, but there were no vacancies. He took up cheap lodgings at the Rainbow Tavern in North Bridge, and pursued both employment and women with what he considered a Parisian flair. He was rejected on both counts, and would again exhibit near suicidal histrionics when the object of his affections rejected him. His self-destructive acts were not taken seriously and were considered by friends as merely for show. He even wrote to his sister, Anastasie, "I would never commit suicide unless I could be there to contemplate it."

At the start of 1852, after months of temporary jobs, Emile's luck and charm paid off once again when William Pringle Laird offered him permanent work and lodging at his nursery in the city of Dundee.

Emile soon discovered, however, that Dundee was too similar to the slow pace of Jersey, and he believed working once again in a nursery to be a step backward from the sophisticated lifestyle he craved. He also discovered that his former beloved in Fife was engaged to another. Only six months after arriving in Dundee, he announced that he would soon be moving on to Glasgow. His charm had worked well in those six months, however, as Laird promised Emile that a job and lodgings at the Dundee nursery would always be available to him.

He packed his few belongings, wished his employer and the Laird family farewell, and traveled southwest to Glasgow, where his fate awaited him.

Several years earlier, while the young Emile was in the early years of his apprenticeship on Jersey, a girl was born nearly five-hundred miles north, to the wealthy Glasgow architect James Smith and his wife, Elizabeth. It was their first child, and the baby was baptized Madeleine Hamilton Smith, the middle name in honor of her maternal grandfather, David Hamilton, the famous architect and mastermind of Glasgow's Royal Exchange and the Western Bank on Miller Street.

Like Emile, Madeleine became the oldest of five children, followed by her sister, Bessie, named after her mother; a brother, John, called Jack; another sister named Janet; and finally James, named after his father.

The Smith family lived in a large and stylish house on India Street in one of the more prosperous areas of Glasgow. As a daughter of an upper-class family, Madeleine was educated from her earliest years in the proper manners and culture of one of the gentry. Class separation was a strictly enforced concept in mid-nineteenth-century Glasgow, and Madeleine, almost from birth, accompanied her parents to the parties and other social occasions worthy of one of her status. With her large gray eyes and dark, rich hair, she was noticed at every function she attended, and was soon a well-respected girl among the Glasgow elite.

When she came into her early teens, she traveled to London to attend Mrs. Gorton's Academy for Young Ladies, located on Upper Clapton Road. For reasons no longer known, James Smith felt that only England could provide a proper education for his daughter, and he turned his back on the many fine schools in Scotland.

Madeleine joined a group of seventeen girls under the leadership of Mrs. Alice Gorton, and the daily regimen was strict: early prayers, breakfast, piano lessons, walking as exercise, lessons on current events, tatting and other ladies' crafts, and training in proper manners. Any free time the students had was to be used for devotions or other activities suitable for young ladies. There were occasional trips to local events and cultural festivities, including the Great Exhibition at Hyde Park. Events of worldwide importance, such as the funeral of the Duke of Wellington and the French Revolution of 1848, were discussed by Mrs. Gorton's pupils. These events and other gossip were dutifully reported by Madeleine in twice-weekly letters to her parents.

Madeleine proved herself to be a good but not outstanding student. Mrs. Gorton remarked to James and Elizabeth that their daughter was well behaved and intelligent but subject to "stubborn sulks" and other flares of temper.

Madeleine graduated and then returned to the India Street house in the summer of 1853, going quietly back into the life of a daughter of one of the gentry. She once again accompanied her parents to social gatherings, including a party near Govan Village where she reportedly wore white silk stockings, a "fetching Tarlatan dress," and her hair in falling ringlets. Often during the course of the year, and for most of the summer, the Smith family left Glasgow and retired to their sprawling country house, Rowaleyn, at Row (now known as *Rhu*), twenty-five miles up the River Clyde from Glasgow.

There is no reason to believe that the Smith family interacted any better or worse than other upper-class families, although in later letters, Madeleine would betray negative feelings about her parents and siblings: "I love them, for they have been kind to me. But I must confess I fear them. I could not confide in Father, Brother, Mother, Sister. I fancy they are the most indulgent parents, yet there is an awe which should not be." Her father dominated the house and family, and her mother quietly enacted her husband's will. Madeleine would write of her mother: "[she] is very good, but you cannot make a confidante of her. I could not open my heart to her."

By the time Madeleine returned home from Mrs. Gorton's school, Emile was settled into Glasgow. He set up lodgings in a boarding house on Kingston Place, in a working-class neighborhood on the south side of the Clyde. He searched unsuccessfully for work, until he accidentally came across an elderly woman who remembered him fondly from his days at Dicksons and Company in Edinburgh. She arranged a position for him as a warehouse clerk with Huggins and Company, merchants with offices at 10 Bothwell Street.

Soon after Emile started work, though, news arrived from Jersey that his only brother, Achille, had died and his mother was inconsolable. Lacking the funds to return home, and not wanting to ask for leave from Huggins so soon after beginning his employment, Emile sent his heartfelt condolences to his family but remained in Glasgow, carving out a life for himself.

Emile's amiable manner once again attracted his coworkers and neighbors. His friends ranged in social status from Tom Kennedy, the cashier at Huggins, to Monsieur August de Mean, the Chancellor of the French Consulate in Glasgow.

In order to cultivate the personal contacts needed to further his social aspirations, Emile took time deciding on the church he would regularly attend. He realized that church was a prime vehicle for meeting people, and, although born and baptized a Catholic, he knew that the Roman church was not, in general, looked upon with favor in Scotland at that time. Possibly after observing the people who went into the various houses of worship, he began attending St. Jude's Church on Jane Street, the only Episcopalian church in Glasgow.

As a stranger among the parishioners, Emile received curious looks the first few Sundays, but he made an effort to talk to people before and after services, and soon included several of the congregation in his ever-growing number of friends.

Foremost of the friendships he established at St. Jude's was with the matronly Mary Arthur Perry, the unmarried daughter of a drysalter who lived alone in her father's large house on West Renfrew Street. Her own life was relatively quiet, but Miss Perry lived vicariously through the lives of her many friends—becoming an intimate advisor in their personal problems and decisions.

Soon after their introduction, Miss Perry gently told Emile that his lodgings at Kingston Place (on the southern side—and therefore "wrong" side—of the Clyde River) were not the sort for a gentleman wanting to move within proper society. Miss Perry enlisted the aid of the reverend of St. Jude's, and together they found a vacancy in the house of Peter Clark, curator of the Royal Botanic Garden. Mr. Clark's house was on the northern side of the Clyde, on the Great Western Road and at the edge of the Garden. It was an affordable place for Emile, and one that would be acceptable to his circle of friends. Emile moved in during May of 1854. He would live there for more than two years, before his next (and final) move into the boarding house of Mrs. Ann Jenkins.

Part III

The 1855 Correspondence

HISTORY IS SILENT on the subject of when Emile L'Angelier first saw Madeleine Smith. Her family occasionally made outings to the Botanic Garden, although he may have first seen her among the throng of busy shoppers on Sauchiehall Street, one of Glasgow's primary shopping districts. Regardless of where and when the encounter took place, he was instantly attracted to her, and his former habit of relentlessly pursuing a specific young lady resurfaced.

As Madeleine was a member of one of Glasgow's most prominent families, it would have been easy for Emile to discover who she was. Even the lower classes, who never actually interacted with the Smiths, would know them by sight. Once aware of her identity, most other men would have seen the impossibility of forming a relationship with a young lady of such social standing, and would have gone off in other pursuits. But Emile was not like most other men. Once able to attach a name to her attractive face, he began to search for a way to speak to her.

The strict rules of Victorian society forbade a gentleman from simply walking up and speaking with a lady—he needed to be introduced by a mutual acquaintance. As Emile and Madeleine were several levels apart on the social strata, the chances of them knowing someone in common was slight, and it took Emile many weeks to find such a connection. He eventually fell upon the knowledge that a coworker had two nephews, Charles and Robert Baird, who were acquainted with the Smith family. With his goal firmly in mind, Emile soon arranged to be invited to the Baird family home on Royal Crescent. Once in their company, Emile set about trying to enlist one or both of the brothers in introducing him to Madeleine. Emile found Charles, the elder of the two, too savvy to work with, so he concentrated his efforts on seventeen-year-old Robert. Emile boldly proposed an introduction, but Robert felt hesitant and asked his uncle, Emile's coworker, to do the introduction. The uncle, not knowing the Smith family himself, refused. Emile then suggested that Robert ask his mother to arrange a dinner to which both Madeleine and Emile would be invited. The mother, finding this an odd request, also refused. Undaunted, Emile continued formulating ways to meet the dark-haired young lady.

Fortune struck one day in late February or early March of 1855, as Emile and Robert were walking together down Sauchiehall Street and saw Madeleine and another young lady go into Paterson's Draper's Shop. Emile told Robert to go inside and bring Madeleine out and introduce her to him. If Robert was reluctant, Emile eventually coerced him; and so on that chilly day in the spring of 1855, Madeleine and the other young lady, her sister, Bessie, came out onto the steps of Paterson's, and the two sisters met the handsome dark-haired gentleman with the slight accent.

It is not recorded what conversation passed between them, but Emile must have made a strong impression on young Madeleine. Soon after their introduction, the two met in bookstores and other public places, and occasionally walked together along the streets of Glasgow. Emile once gave Bessie a note to be passed to Madeleine.

The days became warmer and the Smith family left Glasgow for their summer home of Rowaleyn. Mr. Smith stayed in Glasgow when necessary for his business, but joined the family at Row whenever he could. Social calls during the summer months occasionally required the entire family to return to Glasgow for a brief interval.

From Rowaleyn, Madeleine sent Emile the first in what would become an enormous volume of letters.

> MY DEAR EMILE,
>
> I do not feel as if I were writing you for the first time. Though our intercourse has been very short, yet we have become as familiar friends. May we long continue so. And ere long, may you be a friend of Papa's—that is my most earnest desire.
>
> We feel it rather dull here after the excitement of a town's life. But then, we now have much more time to devote to study and improvement. I often wish you were near us. We could take such charming walks. One enjoys walking with a pleasant companion, and where could we find one equal to yourself?
>
> I am trying to break myself of all my very bad habits—it is you I have to thank for this, which I do sincerely from my heart.
>
> Your flower is fading.

"I never cast a flower away,
The gift of one who cared for me.
A little flower, a faded flower,
but it was done reluctantly."

I wish I understood botany for your sake, as I might send you some specimens of moss. But alas, I know nothing of that study.

We shall be in town next week. We are going to the Ball on the 20th of this month, so we will be several times in Glasgow before that. Papa and Mama are not going to town next Sunday. So, of course, you must not come to Row. We shall not expect you.

Bessie desires me to remember her to you.
Write on Wednesday or Thursday.
I must now say adieu.

With kind love, believe me, yours very sincerely,
MADELEINE.

Madeleine's letters to Emile have always proven problematic for her biographers. Many are undated or dated solely by the day of the week. Her use of lengthy phrases of endearment was excessive, her handwriting harsh and overly florid, and her punctuation was lazy. Her final letter to Emile, in fact, contained no punctuation whatsoever. Often, when she finished with a page, she would turn the paper sideways and write over what she had already written, instead of using a clean sheet. Her letters are integral for providing an in-depth character study of Madeleine (and, to a lesser extent, of Emile), and are presented herein in what appears to be the correct chronological order, although they have been edited for brevity and to avoid repetition.

From her first letter, two themes that would indelibly mark their entire relationship were already firmly in place: Emile's attempts to mold Madeleine into something of his design, by correcting all of her "bad habits"—and the strict scheduling of when they could and could not meet face to face. Arrangements for the latter would become increasingly complex and deceitful as time went on.

By the time Madeleine wrote her next letter, James Smith had found out about Madeleine's friendship with Emile and had not been pleased. Rather than confront her father's objections head-on, which a proper Victorian daughter would not do, Madeleine devised the first in a long series of deceptive strategies.

April 3, 1855

MY DEAR EMILE,

Many thanks for your last kind epistle.

We are to be in town tomorrow. Bessie said I was not to let you know—but I must tell you why! Well, some "friend" was "kind" enough to tell Papa that you were in the habit of walking with us. Papa was very angry with me for walking with a gentleman unknown to him. I told him we had been introduced, and I saw no harm in it. Bessie joined with Papa and blames me for the whole affair. She does not know I am writing you, so don't mention it.

We are to call at our old quarters in the Square on Wednesday about quarter past twelve. So if you could be in Mr. McCall's Lodgings and see us come out of Mrs. Ramsay's—come after us. Say that you are astonished to see us in town without letting you know. And we shall see how Bessie acts. She says she is not going to write you.

We are to be in town all night. We are to be with Mrs. Anderson.

Rest assured—I will not mention to anyone that you have written me. I know from experience that the world is not lenient in its observations. But I don't care for the world's remarks so long as my own heart tells me I am doing nothing wrong.

Only if the day is fine expect us tomorrow. Not a word of this letter.

Adieu till we meet. Believe me, yours most sincerely,
MADELEINE.

Bessie, who had asked to be remembered to Emile in the first letter, was now instructing Madeleine not to make plans to meet with Emile again. Whether Bessie was jealous, thought Madeleine's relationship with Emile was improper, or was the "friend" who informed Mr. Smith is not known. The cryptic "I know from experience that the world is not lenient in its observations" is not explained, but most likely refers to some past gossip of which upper-class people like Madeleine were often the subject.

Despite Bessie's admonishment, Madeleine did not always view her sister as strict and puritanical. Madeleine would write:

I shall do all I can to prevent my sister being fast. . . . At one time we tried to make ourselves conspicuous and we liked to be talked of by gentlemen. Bessie and I did succeed in that and I assure you I am sorry for it now. Bessie still likes to be talked of. A young gentleman . . . told her on Sunday night that she was spoken a good deal of, and not in the best way—meaning she was a flirt—and she told him she was delighted to hear it and that she would do all in her power to get more spoken of. Fine character, this! I am sorry for her—but she will live to regret it all, as I have done.

The topic of Emile apparently came up several times at Rowaleyn during the spring of 1855. We cannot know the extent of the pressures the Smith family put on Madeleine, and although she was as stubborn as that society would allow its young women to be, the family's continual disapproval is apparent from her next letter. Following a rendezvous with Emile, probably in Glasgow, Madeleine made her first attempt to break off their correspondence.

April 18, 1855

My Dear Emile,

I now perform the promise I made in parting to write you soon. We are to be in Glasgow tomorrow. But as my time shall not be at my own disposal, I cannot fix any time to see you. Chance may throw you in my way.

I think you will agree with me in what I intend proposing: that for the present the correspondence had better stop. I know your good feeling will not take this unkind, it is meant quite the reverse. By continuing to correspond, harm may arise. In discontinuing it, nothing can be said. It would have afforded me great pleasure to have placed your name on my list of correspondents. But as the song says, "There is a good time coming—only wait a little longer."

If I do not see you in Glasgow, I shall be happy to receive an answer to this—addressed to the Post Office for "Miss Richard." I shall be at the Post Office on Saturday the 28th and will get it on that day.

I shall now bid you adieu for the present—hoping that when we meet it may be as friends, and believe me yours sincerely,
Madeleine H.S.

Emile's response to the fictitious "Miss Richard" must have been persuasive. For the first time since the "Lady from Fife," he was unwilling to play his habitual role of the abandoned suitor, and suggested his seeking a direct introduction to her father.

Five days after her previous letter, Madeleine reversed her position and took up the correspondence again—but insisted upon strict secrecy.

April 23, 1855

MY DEAR EMILE,

Accept my thanks for your very kind and flattering note. You must have discovered that I have a great regard for you, or I should not have acted as I have done. If I can promote your happiness in the least, believe me, I shall be most willing to do so.

> *Why should I blush to own I love?*
> *Tis love that rules the realm above.*
> *Why should I blush to say to all,*
> *That virtue holds my heart in thrall.*

Do not, at present, get an introduction to Papa. Dear Emile, all this must remain a profound secret. Mention my name to no one. This I ask as a favor. I shall depend on your honor.

By the end of April or soon thereafter, Madeleine had fallen in love with Emile. She would write graphically of her affection for him, eventually corresponding with a frankness that was unthinkable in that era. The place of young women in Victorian times was excessively rigid, and the role of a proper upper-class daughter was one in which Madeleine never felt comfortable. Her relationship with Emile was daring and hidden, and breathed excitement into her otherwise monotonous existence of rules and manners—this may be the sole reason that Madeleine found Emile so attractive, and why she dedicated so much of her life to him.

Both knew that their relationship could become public knowledge only after Emile had been introduced to Mr. Smith and had convinced the older man that a clerk living in a rented room would be an acceptable suitor for his daughter, who spent her days amongst servants and the Glasgow elite.

> I shall never be able to introduce you to Papa. It must be a stranger. So how are we to manage it? I don't know. I have thought of it night and day. We must have patience.
>
> I practice my music every day. But I do not sing—I only play duets with Bessie.
>
> Emile, do not ask for a lock of my hair. Any other thing I will give you, but not a lock of hair. I promised to one who is now in the cold grave I should never give a second lock of hair—and a promise to the dead is sacred. Do not blame me for refusing it—even to you whom I love so dearly.

Throughout the summer of 1855, Emile occasionally traveled by ferry to Row and met Madeleine secretly, late at night, in the woods surrounding the

Smith home. He brought her small gifts of jewelry and his ambrotype portrait. During one of her brief stays in Glasgow, Madeleine managed to sneak away and have tea with Emile at Miss Perry's house. Letters continued back and forth between the two, and the relationship escalated to the point where Emile told Miss Perry that the two were engaged, their marriage planned for September of 1856.

During that summer of 1855, Emile took a brief furlough from Huggins and visited his family in Jersey. Before he left, Madeleine wrote him a quick note:

DEAR, DEAR EMILE,

I am sure you must feel very happy at the prospect of so soon seeing your Mama and sister. They must be very fond of you. Who could not but love my own sweet Emile? At least I fancy no one could but love you. I never saw anyone I could love as I do you. Though I appear cool, yet I love you with all my heart and soul.

You shall have a lock of my hair. When I refused it at first, we were not engaged. Now we are and you have a right to ask anything from me.

A large obstacle to Emile's marriage to Madeleine was financial. He earned a meager salary at Huggins and there was little hope for advancement. Knowing that Madeleine was used to the finest in life and that her parents, solidly against their union, would provide no monetary support if they married, Emile searched for a solution. The situation brightened during his short visit to Jersey. Bernard Saunders, whom Emile had apprenticed to, told him of an acquaintance with a market-garden outside of Lima, Peru, who was looking for a dependable man to oversee the manual labor and business of the place. A fine house and a good salary would be part of the package. Emile, seeing a way of simultaneously making money and escalating up the social ladder, asked Saunders and his family to write enthusiastic letters of reference for him. He then wrote Madeleine a brief letter, outlining his plans for the two of them.

Emile's mother was horrified at the prospect of her son living halfway around the world. Madeleine was similarly upset:

I have just received your note. What a shock that note has given me! Oh, what must I do? Tell me dearest—I have only you to give me advice. Would to God we had been married—as the lady you told me of. Then no power on earth could have prevented me accompanying you to Lima. Though it is a great distance, I would go any place with you, my beloved Emile. If you go—then I know I shall never see you more. I may bid you farewell forever. Ah! Forever. Will nothing prevent you from going? You will never stand the climate—it will kill you. Oh, dearest of my soul, could not you do Europe? I would leave all to go with you.

Madeleine, still in the initial phases of love for Emile, considered their relationship a sweet secret to lighten her dull life. His going to Peru would end that, and her mind raced with ideas to keep him in Glasgow. In her next letter, almost as a bribe, she presented a scheme for Emile to meet her father. She also used, for the first time, the nickname *Mimi* which, along with *Mini*, would appear in her letters to Emile and Miss Perry.

MY DEAREST EMILE,

How I long to see you. It looks an age since I bid you adieu. Will you be able to come down the Sunday after next? You will be back in Glasgow by the 14th.

I hope you have given up all idea of going to Lima. I will never be allowed to go to Lima with you—so I shall fancy you want to get quit of your Mimi. You can get plenty of appointments in Europe—any place in Europe. For my sake, do not go.

We are to be very gay all this week, although I am quite tired of company. What I would not give to be with you alone. Oh, would we not be happy? Ah, happy as the day was long.

Give dear Miss Perry my love and a kiss when you write. I love her so. What a friend she would be to us.

I feel very nervous today. My hand shakes so. I have not felt well since I got your last letter, and I try to appear cheerful before my family—and it is not easy to appear in good spirits when there is a pain at the heart.

Adieu for today—if I have time I shall write another note before I post this.

Believe me, your ever devoted and fond,
MIMI.

P.S. Tuesday morning

We can be only one day in Glasgow at the time of the Association. We are to have so many friends that week that we cannot possibly leave. There is to be a "full dress" meeting in the McLelland Rooms on the 13th. I think Papa would like it if we go, but I have not made any arrangements as yet. If I thought you were to be there, I would go. Though I could not speak to you, yet I would see you. You would try and get an introduction to Papa that evening. He would be sure to be in good temper. Let us hope.

A kiss. Your true fond,
MIMI.

The combined pressure from Madeleine and his mother dissuaded Emile from pursuing the position in Peru. He wrote Madeleine, probably telling her that his decision to abandon the job was out of love for her. As reciprocation, he urged her to once again ask for her family's acceptance of him as a suitor. Madeleine knew her parents' position and declined.

After his return to Glasgow, Emile continued to press the point, and probably made at least one late-night visit to Rowaleyn. His protestations eventually won her over, and Madeleine promised to confront her parents once again. She wrote Emile with her strategy for facing her father, coached him for what she considered to be an inevitable meeting between the two men, and painted a dark sketch of her father, who was expected back at Row during the coming week.

> I intend to be very decided with Papa. Tell him I will never marry any other one but Mr. L'Angelier. I shall try and bear with all the threats he will hold, but I am not easily frightened. He will find out that his daughter has a mind of her own. . . .

> I shall write Papa on Monday so he will get it on Tuesday. He will most likely send for you. Be firm. Be careful what you tell him. I shall tell him I receive letters from you at the Post Office. . . . I shall tell him you have no fortune, but ere long you hope to have one. If he cannot give his consent then what shall I do? For I could not see you go away! No, you must not go alone. We will succeed yet—I am sure. I often think of the others who have won through—so why not me? It would be better if we were out of Scotland, for I know there will be no great pleasure with my friends after. Don't show him any of my letters. Destroy them all. Nobody shall ever see mine from you. I shall mention to Papa that you tried to get an introduction but could not. Do keep cool when you see him. I know his temper—[it is] very much like my own.

The week passed. Emile heard no more. There was no summons from James Smith, nor another letter from Madeleine. Emile waited.

What exactly was said between Madeleine and her father in the stately home of Rowaleyn is not known, but the tone and outcome of the conversation are readily apparent in her next letter, dated September 21, 1855.

FAREWELL, DEAR EMILE,

> My Papa will not give his consent. I've given my word of honor I will have no more communication with you.

> Get married. You will never get one who will love you as I have done. I must banish your image from my heart. It almost breaks my heart to re-

turn to you your likeness and chain—I must not keep them. Write me a parting note—the last one I can ever receive.

Go to Lima. May God protect you is my prayer.

As a parting favor, may I ask that you will burn all my letters the day you receive this. Do it.

Be happy. Forget me and may she whom you call your wife be a comfort unto you. May she love and esteem you.

Fare thee well,
MADELEINE.

In the same post, Madeleine sent a short note to Mary Perry.

DEAREST MISS PERRY,

Many kind thanks for all your kindness to me. Emile will tell you I have bid him adieu. My Papa would not give his consent, so I am in duty bound to obey him. Comfort dear Emile. It is a heavy blow to us both. I had hoped some day to have been happy with him, but, alas, it was not intended. We were doomed to be disappointed.

You have been a kind friend to him. Oh, continue so! I hope and trust he may prosper in the step he is about to take. I am glad now that he is leaving this country, for it would have caused me great pain to have met him.

Think my conduct not unkind. I have a father to please, and a kind father, too.

Farewell, Miss Perry, and with much love believe me,
yours most sincerely,
MIMI.

Madeleine once again broke off her relationship with Emile because her family, her father in particular, had ordered it so. Emile never fully comprehended the opposition Madeleine faced from her family regarding her love for a mere warehouse clerk. She would eventually attempt to describe it:

[My father] hates you with all his heart. He despises you . . . he cares not for what I say. Though I tell him my mind is made up, he won't care . . . I do not think he understands the warm love of young people. He has forgotten all his youthful passions. . . .

[My mother] hates you. [She'd] rather see me dead than, beloved, your wife. She shall retract those words. I said she had watched me so that I could never see you. "Yes," she said. "And I shall watch you more strictly yet."

[My brother, Jack] came in to sit with me tonight in my bedroom, and he was telling me all the news he knew. I said, "I wish you would tell me something about a person, the only person I love." "L'Angelier," he said. I was in fun, [so] I said, "No." "Well," he said, "I am ashamed of you. Do you know he is only a clerk in Huggins?" I said I knew that, but "if I love him, then that was enough." He tried to tell me I was expected to marry a rich man—not a poor one. He got a little cross and told me not to think of you, as he knew Papa would be angry, very angry. . . .

[After passing Emile one day on the street] Bessie said, "Your worthy friend hardly looked or bowed to you!" And then . . . I was told "he did it on purpose to give you a hint. . . . I knew it would come to this. I have no doubt that he is after some other girl. So you are cut. *So you are cut!*" I felt too numbed to reply.

The family's opinion even clouded Madeleine's sense of proper manners: "I met Miss Perry on Wednesday with her sister," she once wrote Emile. "I felt so ashamed to meet her. I could not bow—Bessie was with me."

Emile responded to Madeleine's second farewell letter with silence—the single tactic that was guaranteed to completely unhinge Madeleine, although he may not have known this at the time. Within a week, another impassioned letter was posted at Row.

DEAREST EMILE,

For the love of heaven, write to me—if it should only be a line. I know you must hate me. But, oh, forgive me. Write by return post. No one shall know. Perhaps Papa has written you—I know not—telling you never more to write to me. But he shall never know.

I have suffered much. It can't be helped. Hope we may yet be happy.

Yours, MIMI.

Emile's reply is gone, as are all of his letters to Madeleine, but a working draft of his response was found among his possessions after his death. It can be assumed that this copy is similar to the letter he eventually sent.

MADELEINE,

In the first place, I did not deserve to be treated as you have done. How you astonish me by writing such a note without condescending to explain the reasons why your father refuses his consent. He must have reasons, and I am not allowed to clear myself of accusations.

I should have written you before, but I preferred waiting until I got over the surprise your last letter caused me, and also to be able to write you in a calm and collected manner—free from any animosity whatsoever.

Never, dear Madeleine, could I have believed you were capable of such conduct. I thought and believed you unfit for such a step. I believed you true to your word and to your honor.

I will put questions to you which you must answer yourself:

What would you think if even one of your servants had played with anyone's affections as you have done, or what would you say to hear that any lady friends had done what you have?

What am I to think of you now?

What is your opinion of your own self after those solemn vows you uttered and wrote to me?

Show my letters to anyone, Madeleine, I don't care who, and if any find that I misled you, I will free you from all blame.

I warned you repeatedly not to be rash in your engagement and vows to me, but you persisted in that false and deceitful flirtation, playing with affections which you knew to be pure and undivided—and knowing at the same time that at a word from your father, you would break all your engagement.

You have deceived your father as you have deceived me. You never told him how solemnly you bound yourself to me, or if you had, for the honor of his daughter, he could not have asked to break off an engagement such as ours.

Madeleine, you have truly acted wrong. May this be a lesson to you: never trifle with anyone again.

I wish you every happiness. I shall be truly happy to hear that you are happy with another. You desired it, and now you are at liberty to recognize me or cut me just as you wish—but I give you my word of honor I shall act always as a gentleman towards you.

We may meet yet, as my intentions of going to Lima are now at an end. I would have gone for your sake. Yes, I would have sacrificed all to have you with me—and to leave Glasgow and your "friends" you detested so very much.

Think what your father would say if I sent him your letters for a perusal. Do you think he could sanction your breaking your promises? No, Madeleine, I leave your conscience to speak for itself.

I flatter myself that your father can only accuse me of a want of fortune. But he must remember—he, too, had to begin the world with dark clouds round him.

I cannot put it out of my mind that yet you are at the bottom of all this.

How Madeleine responded to this letter is not known. At least one more letter to Emile, now lost, passed between the two, and they may have held another midnight meeting at Rowaleyn. Regardless, some form of reconciliation was reached, as Madeleine's next known letter, which mentions the missing letter, is back to her old style: full of endearments, her detailed sight-seeing plans, and gossip.

My Dearest Own Emile,

Another letter so soon. You will be astonished, I am sure.

But I find that I must go from home. Bessie has changed her mind and won't go—so I must. My brother, Jack, a lady from London, and myself are to take a trip, so I have got the charge of them! This is the short tour I propose: We go in our own carriage to Luss, get the steamer there to Inversnaid, to Loch Katrine, to the Trossachs, to Callendar, to Bridge of Allan. I shall stay there all night. Next morning I shall go to Stirling, and from there I shall go to Glasgow on Friday.

I should so wish to have you with me on this short trip, but perhaps some day we may go over the same ground together. It will neither be my fault or yours if we do not become happy some day.

I passed such a pleasant hour last evening—reading all your dear, kind letters. I began with that little note which you gave to Bessie to deliver to me. I cannot fancy how I became the possessor of it. I often thank God that you gave me that note, or I should not have known you. But I should have come to know you. I am sure, beloved Emile, ever since I became acquainted with you, I have felt much happier than I did before.

The opening of her next letter indicates that Emile has been ill, and seriously enough that Madeleine is concerned for his mortality. The quick transition into her usual carefree mode, however, contradicts this—and so one is left to wonder if she suspected Emile of playing the illness for sympathy. Emile was in England at the time, visiting some friends of his, the Lane family.

My Dearest Emile,

I left you very sad, indeed. What if I should never see you the more? Oh, Emile, the thought is dreadful—for my sake, take care of yourself.

I do feel so happy that I know your dear friend, Miss Perry. I like her very much. I do not wonder at your loving her as you do.

I have been thinking about telling Papa about us [and our engagement]—but I know he would get into a passion and would not listen to a word. You cannot fancy what a dislike he has to you. His reasons, I do not know. He would tell me to put a stop to all intercourse. He would try to break our engagement—but only death shall break that engagement with me. Never shall I take anyone but my own dear Emile and let them call me their wife. Whatever occurs, I shall remain true to the last.

Write me before you leave England. Address it care of "Haggart, James Smith," Rowaleyn, Row—and put a small "M" in the corner. Do not write in your usual hand, in case of Bessie taking it out of the postbag.

Haggart refers to Christina Haggart, a maid in the Smith household whom Madeleine took into her confidence. Christina would often be employed to mail Madeleine's letters to Emile, and Emile would address the envelopes of his replies to Christina, who would then quietly pass them on to Madeleine.

In early autumn of 1855, Madeleine and her family moved back to their Glasgow home on India Street for the duration of the winter, and the clandestine nightly meetings occurred more frequently than they had at Row. Emile only had to walk a few blocks to see Madeleine, and his letters could be placed outside her window at a specified time, instead of being sent through the mail. Meetings were occasionally made more difficult, however, if Madeleine's youngest sister, Janet, chose to sleep in Madeleine's room.

Emile and Madeleine both realized by this time that their wedding would need to be performed in secret; although Emile would still concoct the occasional scheme to be introduced to James Smith. Although lacking an actual ceremony, they now began referring to each other as *husband* and *wife*. The only obstacle that Madeleine could foresee with their clandestine wedding was the required public announcement of the marriage banns several days before the ceremony. These banns would make their intended marriage known before Madeleine was safely out of her father's house. She would suggest methods for getting around them: ". . . those horrid banns are the only drawback. If you could get the man to cry them in church before any of the congregation come in—it seems that [they] are just done in church: that is all that is wanted. . . ."

A letter in early December of 1855 shows Madeleine concerned about their secret marriage and, once again, Emile's health.

MY OWN DARLING HUSBAND,

I am afraid I may be too late to write you this evening, so as all are out I shall do it now, my sweet one.

I did not expect the pleasure of seeing you last evening—of being fondled by you, dear, dear Emile.

Our cook was ill and went to bed at ten—that was the reason I could see you. But I trust ere long to have a long, long interview with you.

I was at St. Vincent Street today. Bessie and Mama are gone to call for the Houldsworths and some others.

Do go to Edinburgh and visit the Lanes. Also, my sweet love, go to the Ball given to the officers.

I think you should consult Dr. MacFarlan—that is, go and see him, get him to sound you, tell you what is wrong with you. Ask him to prescribe for you—and if you have any love for your Mimi, follow his advice and do not try to doctor yourself—but follow the doctor's advice. Be good for once, and I am sure you will be well.

I did, my love, so pity you standing in the cold last night, but I could not get Janet to sleep—little stupid thing.

This is a horrid scroll, as I have been interrupted twice by that boring visitor.

I can say nothing as to our marriage, as it is not certain when my parents may go from home or when I may go to Edinburgh. It is uncertain. Will we require to be married in Edinburgh, or will it do here? You know I know nothing of these things. I fear the publishing of the banns in Glasgow, there are so many people who know me. If I had any other name but Madeleine, it might pass—but it is not a very common one. But we must manage in some way to be united ere we leave town.

If ever I again show temper—which I hope to God I won't—don't mind it. It is not with you I am cross.

When may we meet again? Soon I hope and trust.

My own Emile, I wish to get this posted tonight, as I don't understand the post. I posted your Saturday note before noon, and you did not get it till Monday. We have had a great many letters go astray lately. I got a letter on Monday morning written six weeks ago!

How are your mother and sister? Well, I hope, my sweet.

But, pet, I must stop, as they will be in shortly. If I do not post this tonight, you shall have a P.S.

Much love—I am thy ever fond wife,
thy MIMI L'ANGELIER.

Part IV

The 1856 Correspondence

THE LONG WINTER CONTINUED with an ongoing exchange of letters and furtive meetings at the large house on India Street. Depending on the time of day and whether Janet slept in Madeleine's room, which was advantageous because it had its own fireplace, Madeleine could occasionally take Emile into the house after the household was asleep. At other times, they whispered to each other through her bedroom window. Meetings required much planning, as evidenced by Madeleine's outline for one: "I shall stay in [one afternoon]. I shall send out the three servants and only keep Christina [Haggart] at home. You will come in by the back door which I shall order to be opened for you, and we shall spend an hour and a half of happiness."

Christmas and the New Year passed, and in January of 1856, she wrote Emile in a masochistic tone:

> I would so like to be in your lodgings for a week unknown to you—just to see how you get on, so that I might do just the same when we go together. I shall not know one thing you like or dislike. It shall be a little difficult at first, but remember, darling, I shall trust to your telling me all these little things at the very first. You must begin with me as you intend to end: give me a good blow up whenever you have a little time or nothing else to do.

Later that month, the opportunity for a brief meeting presented itself, and Madeleine wrote Emile with her detailed plan for the rendezvous and also told of the latest drama in the Smith household.

> You come to India Street at half past ten. Go on the opposite side. I shall open the curtain of the dining room window. If I do so, then come over to

the door and if all is clear, I shall have it open for you to walk in. I hope it will be all right. We shall have an hour at least.

There has been a horrid affair in the house tonight. Our cook's clothes took fire, and she is much burnt: the arms and face. I was the only one who could help the doctor to dress it. I dressed it myself for the second time at twelve o'clock tonight. But after I did it, I fainted! The first time I ever fainted. I was so sorry . . . it looked so stupid to have so little nerve.

Excuse the pencil—I am writing at the breakfast table. Papa beside me—thinking I am putting down the day's order! Mama goes to Row, so, dearest, come this evening. I hope all shall end well, and we shall pass an hour together.

But I must stop, for the *Old Gentleman* is moving about the room.

The early months of 1856 passed with Emile's life of work and small entertainments continuing to be a sharp contrast to Madeleine's dances and the elegant events of the Glasgow social season. Spring came and the Smiths returned to Row. It had been approximately one year since their introduction and first letters, and Madeleine noted the anniversary in a letter to Emile.

It is a year today—by the day of the week—since you gave me *the* note. I thought of it this afternoon. Do you remember I left Bessie and went with you? She was angry, but I was not. If I had not gone, you might have never given me that dear, dear note, and this night I might not have been your intended wife. I had not the least idea what [the note] was. I wore it next [to] my heart at the Ball that night. Every thought that night was of you.

This pleasant time of romantic reminiscence was soon broken at Row, as the topic of Emile came up once again between Madeleine and her mother. Mrs. Smith may have always harbored suspicions about the continuation of the forbidden relationship, as Madeleine had once written: "Christina is asked very often if there are any letters from you [to me]. Of course, she says 'no.' All my letters are taken to Mama before I get them. That used not to be."

Madeleine detailed the particulars regarding the latest encounter with her mother in a March 4, 1856 letter.

DEAREST EMILE,

What a lecture I have had. I cannot tell you, dearest, what I have suffered this night. I was told by Mama—Papa is not at home and knows nothing of it—that she knew Papa would rather see me in my grave than your wife. I was told you were poor and but a clerk and that I should look higher. You were called all that was bad. I asked for proofs. She told me I should never be your wife with their consent. I said I intended to be your wife—nothing would change me. I told her of the love I bore you. She said she was ashamed to hear me say I loved you. She wept—she begged of me to give you up. I was firm. I said never another's would I be. I said as soon as I was of age, I would have your letters to me delivered to the house. She said if I was some heiress, I might talk that way, but your letters I would not have. Also, that she would take care the postman did not give me your letters at the post office. She thinks I got them at the post office last year while at Row. She told me the anger of Papa would be fearful—even she would be afraid of it. She implored me with tears to give you up. It cut me to see my mother so. I felt I owed her my life. I love you. I love her. But the love for you rises far above the love for her.

I am never to be allowed out by myself all this summer.

Mama said I often came into the breakfast room like as if I had never [slept]. I was the picture of unhappiness—she knew not the cause—but this explained all. She had no suspicion of me till Bessie came from Edinburgh and told her she had seen you there. Then she thought you must have known I was there. She has given me till after I come back from Edinburgh to fix what is to be the end of this.

Husband, dearest, one thing I shall propose. I know you won't like it. But I must do something to have a little peace and happiness. Would you consent to drop our correspondence till September when we shall be married? You must think this cool of me. But if you wish me to live, I must have some happiness. If I continue to correspond, I shall be dead with misery ere September. This is a horrid plan, but, darling, what must I do? Can you trust me till then? The time shall pass quickly—Emile, I shall be thine in September. God knows I shall never be the wife of another. After our freedom, how could I? No, never. I am your wife. . . .

I promise I shall not play billiards. They have been playing cards tonight—one or two of Jack's friends were in. But I was in no state of mind to be in the Drawing Room. I have not touched a card since you asked me not to do it.

Madeleine attempted to break off the correspondence once again, although she may have intended to continue their secret meetings. Emile refused to give an inch. He persuaded Madeleine, in person and/or by letter, to continue their correspondence.

Madeleine's next letter, on the occasion of his thirty-third birthday, showed her back to her usual form: outlining for Emile the Smith family's guests and her plans for her leisure time.

April 30, 1856

My Own, My Beloved Emile,

I wrote you Sunday night for you to get my note on your birthday, but I could not get it posted. Disappointment it was to me—but "better late than never." May you have very, very many happy returns of this day—and each year may you find yourself happier and better than the last—and may each year find you more prosperous than the last. I trust, darling, that on your next birthday I may be with you to wish you many happy returns in person. May you, dearest, have a long life.

On Sunday I was at church, and in the afternoon Jack and I had a walk of four miles. Now, when I can walk four with a brother, I could walk eight with my own beloved husband and not be fatigued. Yes, darling, we shall take very long walks.

Papa is not at all well and very cross, and he won't go to bed and get better. So I tell him he deserves to be ill.

Tomorrow Houldsworth, Sr., is to be with us, and some more old gentlemen I don't know, and a good many of the Row people [will be here] to dinner. On Monday we are to have a host of friends from Perthshire. I cannot tell you how tired I am of friends! I wish we were more alone.

Friday is a holiday, so James and Janet are to come down on Thursday. Poor Jack cannot get away now. Do you know the office he has gone to work for—McClelland on Ingram Street?

Have you heard from [Monsieur] de Mean since his marriage? I see by the papers he was not married in church. Why not? I don't like marriages in the house. I have never seen a marriage in Scotland. I have been to many in London, though.

Dearest, how I picture our marriage day! Where would you like to go the day we are married? I don't fancy a place in particular, so you can fix that when the time comes. I hope it may yet turn out to be in September. I asked Papa if I were to be married if the banns would be in the church here at Row. And he said no, I had nothing to do with the Row parish—I did not belong to it. So, darling, [the wedding] would not require to be [done] here [in Glasgow]—it *could* never be here—it would not do. I don't in the least mind if they won't give their consent, for I know very well they shall be the first to give in.

I have got my *Chambers Journal* for this month, and the article you mentioned is not in the April issue, so it shall be in the May one. I have been reading *Blackwood* for this month. *Blackwood* is a favorite publication, in fact I think it is the best conducted monthly publication. I have only [begun reading] of Henry VIII in Hume, and I agree with you it would not make a careless person become good. But it is a well-written history. Have you read Macauley's third and fourth volumes? I am rather fond of comparing different authors on the same subject, so I am at present comparing Alison, Hume, and Macauley.

Only fancy, in turning out an old box yesterday, I got a three-year-old notebook, and in going over it, many of the pages had the name "L'Angelier" on them. Now, that is long before I knew you. I did not think I had been so fond of my darling then. I put it in the fire, as there are many names in it I would not like to see beside yours, my own sweet darling husband.

Now this is a very long letter tonight. I must conclude with a fond, fond embrace—a dear sweet kiss. I wish it were to be given, not sent.

The episode of the "three-year-old notebook" is puzzling, as Madeleine did not know Emile three years before the date of the above letter (which she admits), so she could not have written his name down in the book. She either mistook the age of the notebook, previously knew somebody else with the surname L'Angelier (which is doubtful), or left out some explanatory details of the story in her letter.

How Emile actually celebrated his thirty-third birthday is not known. It would be his final birthday.

The weather in the spring of 1856 improved, allowing Emile a visit to Row. Madeleine wrote with specific instructions:

My Own, My Beloved Emile,

The thought of seeing you so soon makes me feel happy and glad. Oh, to hear you again speak to me—call me your own wife—and tell me you love me. Can you wonder that I feel happy?

Papa has been in bed two days. If he should not feel well and come down [to Row] on Tuesday, it shall make no difference—just so that you come. Only, darling, I think if he is in the boat with you, you should get out at Helensburgh instead of at Row. You shall come to the gate—you know it—and wait till I come. I don't think there is any risk. Tuesday, May 6—the gate at half past ten.

I have been rather busy all this week. I have been a great deal out this week, looking after outdoor arrangements. I have got a new employment: the "Hen Yard." I go there every morning. You can fancy me every morning at ten o'clock seeing the hens being fed and feeding my donkey. I don't get on very fast with it—I fear it has little affection. I do for it what I shall, and it only appears to know me, and comes to me when I call.

My beloved Emile, I feel so delighted at the idea of seeing you that I cannot write. I hope you will be able to tell me that we *shall* get married in

September. Nothing shall cause me to break my vows to you. As you say, we are Man and Wife. We shall, I trust, forever remain so.

But I must stop, as Papa wishes me to go and read the papers to him. It is eleven o'clock at night. So if I don't write any more, forgive me, my love.

The May 6 meeting passed, more letters were exchanged, and another rendezvous took place a few weeks later. Subsequent to that late May encounter, Madeleine posted letters to Mary Perry and Emile.

My Dear Mary,

I cannot thank you enough for writing to me in such a free and friendly style as you have done in your last note. I have reason to believe you are a friend indeed.

I was delighted to see dear Emile looking so well—much better than I expected to see him.

My dear friend, it shall be my constant endeavor to practice economy for Emile's sake. I proposed renting lodgings because I thought they would be less expensive than a house, and if there should be a little discomfort attending our residing in lodgings, we must just put up with it for a time. In time, Emile's income shall increase. I don't fear but that we shall get on very well—with economy. I have taken charge of Mama's [household expenses] for the last two years.

I should very much liked to have had a chat with you on these matters, but alas—that is impossible.

It vexes me much to think I have so very few opportunities of seeing my dear Emile. He tries to make up in some measure by being most attentive in writing me. But I must finish.

With kind love, believe me, yours most affectionately,
Mimi.

My Beloved, My Own Darling Emile,

Words can never express to you how truly glad I was to see you last night. Truly last night I did burn with love, but we were good—we withstood all temptations. Some day we may love without fear or trick—we shall then be happy.

When I got in last night I discovered several spots of blood in my clothes. Why was that I wonder?

The "several spots of blood" may have merely indicated that a dark forest is not ideal for a romantic encounter—sharp tree branches and rough underbrush are everywhere—or it could mean that the couple came dangerously close to a taboo that Victorian society strictly forbade and did not even speak of: premarital intercourse.

Madeleine had always been firm in her resolve not to cross that line. She had written Emile: "I shall not yield to you. You shall marry me pure and innocent—as the day on which I was born. You shall never deprive me of my honor. I shall be firm on this point, dearest. I know you shall love me better for it. . . . "

During their next meeting, however, on the night of June 6, 1856, Madeleine and Emile crossed into that forbidden realm. By forming a sexual union, according to the standards of the day, Madeleine could not marry anyone other than Emile, and she could easily have been banished from her father's house. By taking this step, in Victorian society's eyes, her risks were enormous. His were virtually nonexistent.

Her letter to him the following morning, however, betrayed nothing of the shame a proper Victorian young lady would have felt at the event, although it did portray a certain wandering of thought that could possibly be attributed to regret.

Wednesday morning, five o'clock

MY OWN, MY BELOVED HUSBAND,

I trust to God you got home safe and were not much the worse for being out.

Thank you, my love, for coming so far to see your Mimi. It is truly a pleasure to see you, my Emile.

Beloved, if we did wrong last night, it was in the excitement of our love. Yes, beloved, I did truly love you with my soul. Oh, if we could have remained, never more to have parted. But we must hope the time shall come.

I must have been very stupid to you last night. But everything goes out of my head when I see you, my darling, my love. I often think I must be very, very stupid in your eyes. You must be disappointed with me. I wonder if you like me in the least. But I trust and pray the day may come when you shall like me better. Beloved, we shall wait till you are quite ready.

I shall see and speak to Jack on Sunday. I shall consider telling Mama—but I don't see any hope from her. I know her mind. You, of course, cannot judge my parents. You know them not.

I did not know—or I should not have done it—that I caused you to pay extra postage for my stupid, cold letters. It shall not occur again.

Darling Emile, did I seem cold to you last night? Darling, I love you. Am I not your wife? Yes, I am. And you may rest assured after what has passed that I cannot be the wife of another but dear, dear Emile. No—now it would be a sin.

I am sorry you are going to lose your kind friends, the Seaverights. I am so glad when you have kind friends, for then I know you can go there of an evening and be happy. I often think of your long evenings by yourself.

What a happy day [Monsieur] de Mean's marriage day must have been. I have a regret that it was not ours—but the time shall pass away.

I dread next winter. Only fancy: us both in the same town and unable to write or see each other. It breaks my heart to think of it. Why, beloved, are we so unfortunate?

I am sorry for your cold. You were not well last night, I saw you were not yourself. Beloved pet, take care of it.

Emile, beloved, I have sometimes thought: would you not like to go to Lima after we are married? Would that not do? Any place with you, pet.

I did not bleed in the least last night, but I had a good deal of pain during the night.

Tell me, pet, were you angry at me for allowing you to do what you did? Was it very bad of me? We should, I suppose, have waited till we were married.

I shall always remember last night. Will we not often talk of our evening meetings after we are married? Why did you say in your letter: "if we are not married"? Beloved, have you a doubt but that we shall be married some day?

I shall write dear Mary soon. What would she say if she knew we were so intimate? She'd lose all her good opinion of us both—would she not?

My kind love to your dear sisters when you write. Tell me the names of your sisters—they shall be my sisters some day. I shall love them if they are like their dear brother.

I know you can have but little confidence in me. But, dear, I shall not flirt. I do not think it is right of me. I should only be pleasant to gentlemen. Free with none, my pet, in conversation but yourself. I shall endeavor to please you in this. Now, will you tell me, at the end of the summer, if you have heard anything about me flirting? Just you see how good your Mimi shall be. Oh, I see you smile and say to yourself: "but if she has a chance. . . ." Try and trust me.

What a kind letter Mary wrote me. I won't come out in the serious light again—I must have been sad when I wrote her my last letter. I am sorry for it. But you should not have given it to her.

Kindest love from thy own true and ever devoted
MIMI.

Emile's actual response to her letter no longer exists, but once again an initial draft of his reply was found among his possessions. His letter is far more dramatic than hers, and, while admitting the fault to be his, he simultaneously places the burden of shame on Madeleine. He uses their sexual intimacy as yet another way to push for her family's acceptance of him as her suitor, and does not pass up the opportunity to once again point out Madeleine's faults.

MY DEAREST AND BELOVED WIFE, MIMI,

Since I saw you I have been wretchedly sad. Would to God we had not met that night—I would have been much happier. I am sad at what we did. I regret it very much.

Why, Mimi, did you give way after your promises? My pet, it is a pity. Think of the consequences if I were never to marry you. What reproaches I should have, Mimi. I shall never be happy again. If ever I meet you again, love, it must be as at first. I will never again repeat what I did until we are regularly married.

Try your friends once more. Tell your determination. Say nothing will change you, that you have thought seriously of it, and on that I shall firmly fix speaking to Huggins for September. Unless you do something of that sort, Heaven only knows when I shall marry you. Unless you do, dearest, I shall have to leave the country—truly, dearest. I am in such a state of mind I do not care if I were dead.

We did wrong. God forgive us for it, Mimi. We loved blindly. It is your parents' fault if shame is the result—they are to blame for it all.

I got home quite safe after leaving you, but I think it did my cold no good.

I was fearfully excited the whole night. I was truly happy with you, my pet—too much so, for I am now too sad. I wish from the bottom of my heart we had never parted.

Though we have sinned, ask earnestly God's forgiveness and blessing that all the obstacles in our way may be removed from us.

I was disappointed, my love, at the little you had to say—but I can understand why. You are not stupid, Mimi—and if you disappoint me in information, and I have cause to reproach you for it, you will have no one to blame but yourself. I have given you warning long enough to improve yourself. Sometimes I do think you take no notice of my wishes and desires, but say "yes" for mere matter of form.

Mimi, unless Huggins helps me, I cannot see how I shall be able to marry you for years. What misery to have such a future in one's mind.

Do speak to your brother—open your heart to him, and try to win his friendship. Tell him if he loves you he will take your part.

And besides, my dear, if once you can trust him, how pleasant it will be for you and me to meet. I could come over to Helensburgh when you would be riding or driving, or of a Sunday—I could join you in a walk of a Sunday afternoon.

Mimi, dearest, you must take a bold step to be my wife. I entreat you, pet, by the love you have for me—do speak to your mother. Tell her it is the last time you ever shall speak of me to her.

You are right, Mimi, you cannot be the wife of anyone else than me. I shall ever blame myself for what has taken place. I never, never can be happy until you are my own, my dear fond wife.

Oh, Mimi, be bold for once and do not fear them—tell them you are my wife before God. Do not let them leave you without getting their blessing to our being married, for I cannot answer to what would happen.

My conscience reproaches me of a sin that only marriage can efface.

I can assure you it will be many days before I meet such nice people as the Seaverights—especially the daughter. I longed so much to have introduced you to her, to see the perfect lady in her, and such an accomplished young person.

My evenings, as you say, are very long and dreary.

We must not be separated all next winter, for I know, Mimi, that you will be as giddy as the last. You will be going to public Balls, and that I cannot endure. On my honor, dearest, sooner than see you or hear of your running about as you did last winter, I would leave Glasgow myself. Though I have truly forgiven you, I do not forget the misery I endured for your sake. You know yourself how ill it made me—if not, Mary can tell you.

I do not understand, my pet, your not bleeding. For every woman having her virginity must bleed. You must have done so some other time. Try to remember if you ever hurt yourself in washing, etc. I am sorry you felt pain. I hope, pet, you are better. Be sure to tell me immediately if you are ill next time, and if at your regular period.

I was not angry at your allowing me, Mimi, but I am sad it happened. You had no resolution. We should have waited till we were married, Mimi. It was very bad indeed. I shall look with regret on that night. No, nothing except our marriage will efface it from my memory. Mimi, only fancy if it was known. My dear, my pet, you would be dishonored and that by me! Oh, why was I born, my pet? I dread lest some great obstacle prevents our marriage. If Mary did know it, what should you be in her eyes?

For God's sake burn this, Mimi, for fear anything happening to you.

Dearest Mimi, let us meet again soon—but not as the last time. See if you can plan anything for the Queen's birthday. I intend to be in Helensburgh some night to cross over with Miss White to Greenock. I could refuse stopping with them, and come to see you, but I cannot fix the exact day. And I do not know how to let you know except by sending a newspaper to B., and the evening after the date of the newspaper would be the evening I would come—or tell me a better arrangement. Do you not think it would be best to meet you at the top of the garden, same as last summer?

My dear wife, I could not take you to Lima. No European woman could live there. Besides, I would live three or four thousand miles from [that city]—far from any white people—and no doctors if you were ill or getting a baby. No, if we marry, I must stay in Glasgow until I get enough to live elsewhere. Besides, it would cost £300 alone for our bare passage money.

It had been more than a year since their introduction on Sauchiehall Street. Madeleine and Emile had now engaged in every activity of husband and wife except for an actual wedding.

By this stage of their relationship, Emile had clamped down on Madeleine's activities to the point of making her a partial recluse: virtually forbidding her to go to parties or to stroll along the main streets of Glasgow. Madeleine's upper-class life would, by necessity, include these activities, and her social obligations would remain a continual source of tension between the two. Madeleine's family would also wonder about her withdrawal, as she had always greatly enjoyed such social occasions, and could give them no reason for her sudden lack of interest.

The night of their sexual union was soon followed by yet another clash between Madeleine and her mother over the subject of Emile. A letter to Miss Perry briefly outlined the confrontation.

My Dearest Mary,

A thousand thanks for your dear, kind letter and good wishes for my happiness. I hope there are many, many happy days in store for me. I know I shall be happy with my dear Emile. We love each other, and that shall constitute our happiness. I trust the day is not far distant when you shall see us living happily together. I had a conversation with Mama, but I received no hope from her. She shall never consent to our marriage. I told her my mind was made up—nothing would change me. I shall be the wife of dear Emile.

I made him once unhappy. But I vowed I would never do so again by breaking my vows to him.

Dear Mary, nothing, I fear, shall move my parents. They are against our union, and I fear they shall continue so.

I saw you for a moment at the station in Edinburgh.

I cannot see you—so our acquaintance cannot be cultivated at present. We must have patience for a little.

I am going away soon. I shall be deprived of seeing much of Emile. Do give him advice to take care of himself. He is not well at present. The summer may restore him to good health. I trust so. If he would only be kind to himself.

I must conclude.

> Believe me, dear friend, yours most affectionately,
> MIMI.

Madeleine's letters throughout the remainder of the summer of 1856 continued in their previous vein: expressing undying devotion to Emile, speaking of gossip and their upcoming marriage, apologizing for behaviors that he found unsuitable ("How I have reproached myself all week for writing you such unkind letters. Will you, darling Emile, pardon me for them? I was a little annoyed, but it is all over now . . . "), warning him about false rumors involving her and another man, listing all of the things she was willing to give up for him, and reassuring him on a subject about which he was highly anxious—his salary. The meager wages he received from Huggins continually bothered Emile, even though Madeleine had once written him cryptically: "Perhaps if you had been well off, I would not have loved you as I do."

MY OWN, MY DARLING HUSBAND,

We shall be so happy—happy in our own little room. The thought of those days makes me feel happy. If it were not for these thoughts, I should be sad, miserable and weary of this cold, unfeeling, thoughtless world. Wealth is the ruling passion. Love is a second consideration—when it should be the first, the most important.

[Monsieur] de Mean is at home. Papa told me so—he spoke to him. Jack also saw him, and many of the other gentlemen told me they had seen him. How happy he must be—though I think he would have been happier if he and his bride had been in a house by themselves. What do you think, my darling? In our case, I would rather be by ourselves.

I have no news. Friends staying with us—which is a great annoyance to me. I am weary of it now. I did like this way of living at one time, but I hate it now—it makes me long for our own quiet home. . . .

Don't give ear to any reports you may hear. There are several I hear going about regarding me going to get married. Regard them not. . . .

Emile, I wish I could convince you that I love but for you alone. In whatever recreation I am employed, my thoughts are of my own Emile. I am thoughtless, but believe me, I never forget you, my only love.

We have not yet got to Arrochar. Mama won't allow us to leave when we have friends in our home, so I don't know when we may go. I do wish *she* would go, and then I would see you. . . .

My aunt wrote to me this week and she had seen you. She said that you were looking very well and paid you a pretty little compliment—which I won't tell you, my love.

Now, my sweet pet, you are wrong in thinking I am not preparing for our marriage in the least. I am. I have got very many things ready, so don't fear for me. I shall be quite ready by September. If you are, too—happy time!

Once married, I shall be beside you, so if I do anything wrong, and you check me, I shall never, never do it again. I shall be all you could wish. You shall love me and I shall obey you. I shall leave all, sacrifice friends, relations, family—everything for your sake, for the love I have for you. I shall never regret it.

Jack told me he saw Madame de Mean this week, looking so pretty. He must be very happy and so must she. I have never met up with her since her marriage, but I am only in Helensburgh in the morning, and always driving.

I have not been riding. No one knows why I have not been riding—not even Papa or Mama—but I shall tell you. The Wilsons and Mr. Young asked me to allow them to ride with me. I knew you would not like this, and it would cause people to make remarks. I don't think I shall ride this summer—unless it may be with Jack—no other one.

Her continual interest in Madame de Mean's marriage is a clear projection of Madeleine's hopes for her own happy marriage with Emile. The differences, however, between the life of a warehouse clerk's wife and the wife of a consulate would eventually become apparent even to Madeleine's overly romantic mind.

Madeleine continually reassured Emile when suspicions or melancholia got the better of him. Even in the happier times, Emile could become enraged at small mistakes or perceived negligences on her part. She had once hurriedly scribbled:

> Words cannot express the pain your letter of today has cost me. . . . Emile, would I be guilty of cutting you on Monday? Emile, on my honor I swear to you I never saw you! I know not where we even met you! I went to Papa's office with Mama. Were you on the same side [of the street]? I am not shortsighted—but not a day passes that I do not pass some friend [without seeing them]. But there is no excuse for passing my own beloved Emile.

By the summer of 1856, Madeleine knew Emile's temper well, and her letters occasionally contained false words that she felt would curb his anger and cast her in a better light. She once wrote, far too coincidentally, "I used to say there were three things I would like to do: First, to run off [and elope]. Second, to marry a Frenchman. And third, that I would not marry a man unless he had a mustache, and yours is such a nice one."

In late June, Madeleine sent a letter of apology for a transgression concerning a trip Emile had proposed, and once again addressed the topic of Emile's income.

> BELOVED, DEARLY BELOVED HUSBAND,
>
> . . . I shall never cause you unhappiness again. Yes, I shall behave now more to your mind. I am no longer a child. Rest assured I will be true and faithful wherever you are, dear love. My constant thought shall be of my Emile, who is far, far away. I only consent to your leaving if you think it will do you good—I mean, do your health good.
>
> Your income would be quite enough for me—don't for a minute fancy I want you to better your income for me. No, dearest, I am quite content with the sum you named. When I first loved you, I knew you were poor. I felt then I would be content with your lot, however humble it might be. Yes, your home, in whatever place or whatever kind, would suit me. If you only saw me now—I am all alone in my little bedroom—you would never mention your home as being humble. I have a small room on the ground floor, very small, so don't fancy I could not put up in small rooms and with humble fare.
>
> I knew, dearest, you regretted knowing me and being engaged to me during last winter while I was in Edinburgh. Emile, that time was the only period since I have known you in which I felt the least degree of coolness for you. When I saw you angry with me, I felt cool. Nay, more—one day I met you in Glasgow and you looked so cross at me that when I went home I wrote you a note taking farewell of you, as I thought you would be de-

lighted to get quit of me. But something struck me it was unkind of me doing so. I went to bed, I dreamt of you, I fancied you still loved me, and in the morning all my love for you returned. Never again did I feel cool towards you, though I may have made you fancy so by my cool letter, etc.

We shall make up for all the past then by our loving each other with a sincere heart. We shall be the envy of many—of Bessie, I know.

As you ask me, I shall burn your last letter.

It was my cold which prevented my going to Arrochar. I don't know when we may go now—perhaps not at all. I have promised to go to Stirling to pay a visit in August. Bessie had an invitation to go to Edinburgh Castle next week. The Major knew I would not go, so he did not invite me. I don't think [Bessie] will go—Papa won't allow her to go by herself, and I won't go, so I think she will have to stay at home. Which is much better, don't you think so? [My youngest brother] James goes to Edinburgh to school in August. I think he will go far astray while away from home and everyone. But Papa will have all the blame if the boys are not what they should be. Jack is not near so nice as he was.

I think I have answered all your questions. I think I feel better this week. I cannot eat. I have not taken any breakfast for about two months—not even a cup of tea. Nothing till I get my luncheon at one o'clock. I don't sleep much. I wonder, and so does Mama, that my looks are not changed. But I look as well as if I eat and sleep well. I don't think I am any stouter—but you shall judge when next you see me.

But I must go to bed as I feel cold—so good night.

Would to God it were to be by your side, I would feel well and happy then. I think I would be wishing you to *love* me if I were with you—but I don't suppose you would refuse me.

> For I know you will like to love your
> MIMI.

As instructed, Madeleine burned Emile's previous letter to her. She destroyed or returned all of his letters, probably out of fear that others in the Smith household would accidentally come across them.

Excerpts from her next letters, sent in mid-July of 1856, are notable for three reasons: the definite postponement of their September wedding day; the first reference to the Smiths' new Glasgow house in Blythswood Square, a short distance from their former house on India Street; and the earliest mention of the man who would unknowingly unravel the threads that held Madeleine and Emile together—William Minnoch.

Darling, there is an absurd report in town at present—I have heard it from many. R. Anderson told it to Jack that I am to be married to Mr. Minnoch, junior partner of the Houldsworths. He [Minnoch] tried to get a house at Row but could not. And he has taken the flat above us at Blythswood Square. I suppose it is these circumstances which have given rise to it. You, darling, may hear it. . . .

I was rather stupid at our last meeting. But I had a cold and did not feel in good spirits, but I will try to make up for it at our next meeting.

Emile, you have made a rash promise to me in your last letter. You say that if I were dead you shall never marry again. Now this is wrong of you to say so. You will promise me: that if I should die you will marry as soon as you can. Is not a man more happy with a wife? Is she not a happiness and a comfort to him? A solace to him in his sad hours? A help to him in his old age? A blessing to him if he has a family?

I asked Jack yesterday if he had seen you. He said yes, he saw you on Friday in a cab with a lady and gentleman. I asked how you looked, and he said he thought you looked very cross. He has got a very fast look—Jack—of late. He is not improving, and James is just a very bad little fellow, he swears and goes on at a great rate. Papa thinks it clever. But James will be broken in when he goes to school. I think he will be a little blackguard if he goes on at the present style.

We are to have some Edinburgh friends on Friday, so we must be home. Minnoch was here today again. He only left on Saturday and was back again today. He was here for four hours. He brought a little fellow named Weymiss with him. I think Minnoch might have had a little better feeling than to come so soon—knowing that everyone down here has heard the report regarding myself and him—even the people on our own place. Papa and Mama were much displeased with him. They said nothing, but Mama said it was enough to make people think there was something in the report. Say nothing to Minnoch in passing—it will only make him rude if you say anything. . . .

You know I did feel disappointed at our marriage not being able to take place in September. But as it could not, I just made up my mind to be content, and trust that it may be ere long. We shall fix about that our next meeting, which I hope won't be long.

I did laugh at your pinning my little flower to your shirt. I always put your flowers into books in the drawing room—there I can go and look at them at any time.

You know I have wished as much as you [have] to give you my ambrotype likeness, but I have not had the opportunity. I promise you shall have it some day—so that promise won't be broken.

> I am so glad you go and take a walk on Sunday. I would rather you did so as go to church, as I think the country air would do you more good—and you can read prayers by yourself in the evening.

Mr. William Minnoch was a bachelor in his early thirties and a senior staff member of Houldsworth and Company, a Glasgow merchant/importing firm. Madeleine's father met the young man while on business and took a liking to him. James Smith undoubtedly saw an ideal match for Madeleine in Minnoch, and, not knowing that the forbidden relationship between Emile and Madeleine had continued, began inviting Minnoch to their Glasgow home and to Rowaleyn.

Madeleine did not mention Minnoch in her next letters, focusing instead on her health, her upcoming travel plans, Emile's new threats to depart for foreign countries, and the continuation of their sexual union.

> I got home this evening, but with a very bad cold. I feel quite ill to-night—sick and headache . . . I got my feet wet crossing a stream, and had to drive fifteen miles without getting them dried.

> I was much charmed with the fine scenery all about Arrochar on Thursday—a pretty, fine day. We went to the top of Loch Lomond, driving, and had luncheon in one of the beautiful glens—and returned to Arrochar in the afternoon. Our party consisted of some people from Perth I did not know, and the two Griersons—your friend's brothers. . . . [And] I shall tell you something that shall please you, my own sweet husband: I was the only lady of the party who received no kisses from the gentlemen. I would not have done such a thing. And, of course, when I said I would not allow such a thing—no one asked me.

> . . . Emile, if you go away and go into the French Army, you know you will never return to Scotland. And, of course, I am your wife and I can never be the wife of any other one. So my mind is made up, if you go, I shall go where no one shall see me more. I shall be dead to the world. . . .

> . . . How happy I was with you the other night. But we must not indulge again. What if anything was to occur? What would they say? But, darling, it is hard to resist the temptation of *love*. . . .

> . . . I feel, Emile, yours is a true love. The love a husband should have for his wife. You do not flatter me as others do—you tell me when I am wrong. I love you for all this. It is a kindness to me. Thank you, darling, for being so kind to me. . . .

> . . . When we are married, it will be my constant endeavor to please you and to add to your comfort. I shall try to study you, and when you get a little out of temper, I shall try and pet you, dearest—kiss and fondle you.

I shall ever remain true to you. I think a woman who can be untrue ought to be banished from society. It is a most heartless thing. After your disappointment [with the "Lady from Fife"], dearest Emile, I wonder how you could have any confidence in another. But I feel that you have confidence in me, or you would not love me as you do.

Your likeness is such a comfort to me. Whenever I think of my own dear Emile, I go and look at you. I never saw such a good likeness—I love it truly. I owe you very many thanks for it. I shall try and get mine for you. . . .

Bessie told me she saw you. On Sunday, one of the ladies in Mama's carriage saw you and, fancy, she fell in love with your appearance. I do not wonder at that in the least—as I was quite charmed with you when I first saw you. I do not wonder at young ladies admiring you. I feel quite proud at the thought of having such a very nice-looking husband. But it is not only your appearance that makes me feel proud of you—but your superior mind and ways of thinking different from other young men. I look upon "fast" men now with horror!

All our friends left us yesterday. I think Bessie and some of the family are going to the Bridge of Allan this week—on Wednesday to be home on Saturday. Mama does not like me to leave home much—as she says things go all wrong when I am away. She depends too much on me. I can assure you it is not easy work to manage such a large household. I often feel glad that I have been accustomed to housekeeping—as I shall find the use of it some day.

Emile, for unknown reasons, sent Madeleine a letter late that summer with a plan to relocate to Africa. By this time, he knew that silence and abandonment were the two tactics that could most easily trigger Madeleine's fears, so whether he seriously intended to move away is debatable, as he was apparently looking for new lodgings in Glasgow at the same time. In his letter, he cataloged his depression and the misfortunes of his life, and suggested his talking with Minnoch to crush the growing rumors regarding a relationship between the merchant and Madeleine. Madeleine attempted to console him in her own way.

Emile, I am sorry you are ill—I trust to God you are better. For the love of heaven, take care of yourself. Leave town for a day or two. Yes, darling, by all means go to Mrs. McLan's. It will do you much good.

Only: come back to me.

You cannot, will not, leave me, your wife. I will do all you ask—only remain in this country. I shall keep all my promises. I shall not be thoughtless and indifferent to you. I will do anything—I will do all you mention in your letters to please you—only do not leave me or forsake me. I know what awaits me if I do what you disapprove—off you will go. That shall always be in my mind—you'll go, never to return. The day that occurs, I hope I may die. Yes, I shall never look on the face of man again.

. . . You would die in Africa. Your death would be at my hands. God forbid!

I shall take lessons in watercolors. I shall tell you in my next note what I intend to study. It will rather amuse you. I wonder what you would do with one of my drawings—a stupid, black-looking thing.

Papa gave me the dog, Sambo, a Skye breed—and Pedro, which the coachman got for me, is an English breed. They had their names when I got them.

I am sorry to hear that you dislike melons, as they are rather a favorite of mine.

I hope you will get nice new lodgings. I always thought the Gardens were too far away from your office.

I hope we may meet soon. Papa or Mama are not going from home. We intended to go to Arrochar, so it would be no use, your being in the boat. I shall not see you till the nights are a little darker.

I can trust Christina [Haggart]. She will never tell about our meetings. She intends to be married in November. But she may change her mind.

Minnoch left this morning. Say nothing to him in passing. It will only give him cause to say you did not behave in a gentlemanly manner. Do not do it. He said nothing to me out of place, but I was not a moment with him by myself. I did not wish to be alone with him.

We have an old gentleman of eighty-six years in the house just now, and he is trying, as he says, to make love to me. Poor old man—it is wonderful to see him. He has taken a lot of your last kisses from me. But you would not mind that if you saw the poor old man. His brother is here, too—he is only seventy-four. Their name is Bald.

I shall answer your letter the next time I write.

A letter to Miss Perry in the late summer chronicled Madeleine's recent travels in a much more descriptive vein than her letters to Emile had.

DEAREST MARY,

What a length of time since I have written you! But Emile told me you were at Gourock. I hope you enjoyed your visit and felt benefited from the change of air.

They have all gone out driving, and I am obliged to remain at home, as we expect some friends—and it does not look very hospitable for visitors to arrive and find no one to receive them. That is why I am not out.

Were you in Helensburgh one day about ten days ago? I thought it was like you, but I could not say.

My sister and I were at Arrochar last week. I had never been there, and I was quite delighted with the wild Highland scenery. We were on Loch Lomond—it is indeed the Queen of the Scottish Lakes. The water was like a sheet of glass—the sky so blue and clear—in fact, it was more like a picture than reality. Nothing I enjoy so much as fine scenery, and next to the scenery itself comes a fine picture of the same subject.

I have been too busy for some time, so have not had so much reading as I should like. Mama has not been well, and that has occupied a good part of my time. But next week I shall begin a book again, as by that time I think she will be quite convalescent.

I have got two dogs now to make pets of—they are most affectionate. Their great delight is killing rats, and I assure you I gratify them in their desire.

I fear I shall not have the pleasure of seeing you yet this summer, as I know of nothing that shall call me to Glasgow till I come for the winter. I do long to be acquainted with you, and I don't see how it can be managed. I think I must just have patience, and wait for a little time yet. ·

All things may yet end well, but I rather fear dear Emile and I shall have annoyances yet. But we must hope for the best.

> Adieu for the present. With kind love, I am, dear Mary,
> yours affectionately,
> MIMI.

The more cordial tone of her letter to Mary Perry may partially reflect Madeleine's views on which topics were appropriate for women. Like many Victorians, Madeleine considered women to be an inferior gender, although she fully admitted to being a strong individual herself. She would write at one point:

I had a letter this week asking me to take a paper, *The Waverly*. [It is] written by ladies—but I declined as [I] don't like it. It is not to be expected that women can write an interesting paper. I have got a copy of it and it was milk and water writing—you know the style. I have a very poor opinion of my sex. There is no doubt man is a superior being and that is the reason why I think a wife should be guided and directed in all things by her husband. I get few ladies to agree with me. They all think "woman" is as good and clever as a man. I allow there have been many, many clever women. But a book written by a woman never makes the same impression on my mind as one written by a man. I think that women write poetry much better than they do prose. For example, Mrs. Heman's poems are most beautiful.

Madeleine and Emile met the night of August 13, 1856. Emile attempted to renege on his earlier promise to refrain from additional sexual contact until they were legally married. Madeleine refused, although she did state frankly in her letter following the rendezvous that she had not only fully consented to their previous sexual activity but had actually obtained pleasure from it—something unheard of for proper Victorian ladies.

Possibly in retaliation for denying him sexual fulfillment, Emile spoke of yet another proposed relocation: an Australian job offer. As always, Madeleine took this as her cue to outline her devotion to Emile and forecast her desolation if he should leave her.

The nature of their relationship was subtly changing at this point. For the first time, in a series of letters from mid-August, Madeleine pointed out problems with Emile's behavior ("What made me feel a little vexed with you last night was this: you went and brought up the past events of last winter, and that you promised me you would not do . . . ") and with his appearance ("Your hair is so long that it makes you look—now, don't be angry—not near so good looking. Are you cross at me for saying that? No, love, you are not."). Also, almost as an aside, she brought up questions regarding a possible former love of Emile's:

> I shall tell Jack some day you know Miss Dougall, the doctor's daughter in Elembank Place. I remember long, long ago of seeing you meet that young lady in a house opposite to my Aunt's. Whether by appointment or not, I cannot say. Aunt told me then you were engaged to her.

Emile did not like this change in tone and wrote her a brusque letter. Madeleine, showing a rare flare of temper with Emile, wrote him on August 22 with what author Peter Hunt called Madeleine's "list of resolutions."

1. I have not flirted for a long time—so don't you.

2. I shall study water colors if I can get father to allow me.
   I shall study anything you please to name.

3. I shall not go to a Glasgow Ball without asking your consent.
   Is that fair?

4. I cannot promise to go out only twice a week. This I could not promise.

5. I shall go in Sauchiehall Street as little as I can.

6. I cannot promise not to go out with Bessie. I must go out with her when I have no other one—Janet is at school. I do not think it fair of people to speak of Bessie as they do, for she is not so bad. You may have heard many [negative] stories of her—as your friends have misinformed you more than once regarding me—so they may have of her.

7. I shall write to you as often as I can and as long as I can.

My dear husband, I don't suppose you have confidence in my promises, but [I] will do my best to please you in all things.

Emile dropped any plans for leaving the country by the time of his next letter, and he possibly addressed the questions regarding his prior attachment to the young Miss Dougall. In his letter, sent before he left for a short vacation at Badgemore, Emile included a drawing he had made of Madeleine, which he considered to be a flattering portrait. Madeleine did not see it that way, and thought it was a caricature of her. This misunderstanding was resolved by a meeting of some sort.

In her next letter, Madeleine contradicted statements she had made regarding Emile's income and the more dangerous topic of William Minnoch.

My Own Dear Emile,

How I must thank you for your kind, dear letter. Accept a fond embrace and dear kisses and assurances that I love you as much as ever and have never regretted what has occurred.

I forgive you freely from my heart for that picture—never do the same thing again.

Will you not try, when in England, to get some other situation with a larger income? I wish you could get one out of Glasgow. You dislike Glasgow, and so do I. Try and see what you can do while you are away.

If you go on Monday, don't write me again till I tell you. If you do not go, write me—by way of Christina—so as I may not write to Badgemore. I shall not write to Badgemore till the end of the week.

I like Miss Williams's letter. I think she is very nice. I like her ere I have seen her. Excuse me—but I always just say what I think—but I don't like the other young lady. I cannot tell you what it is, but there is something I don't like. I judge much of a person from their letters and handwriting. I may be wrong—she may be nice.

Jack is still in pain with his leg, but quite able to walk with a halt.

What a stupid boy you are! I told you already what I liked in the August *Blackwood*. I shall read the September one on Monday.

I think you should not mind getting a [wedding] ring, but you shall have the size. I am sure I don't know which finger it ought to be. I have never noticed these things.

I did tell you at one time that I did not like William Minnoch, but he was so pleasant that he quite raised himself in my estimation. I wrote to his sisters to see if they would come and visit us next week—also him—but they cannot.

You ask me what I have been reading—well, then, I shall tell you. The lives of Leonardo da Vinci and M. Angelo, also Andrea del Sarto. All first-class painters. I am fond of reading the lives of painters. The life of Andrea del Sarto quite makes me feel melancholy. His life was a life of unhappiness—he was a prey to sorrow—he never knew what it was to be happy—he died early, deserted by all—even by his wife. Yes, by his wife, the one who should have stayed by him—and shared his sorrows and anxieties.

This is such a horrid cold night. The wind is howling—and rain—it makes me feel so sad. There are two things I dislike: the noise of waters and the wind. Perhaps you may like them both—do you, love?

After I am your wife, I shall be obliged to sign my name as Madeleine Mimi L'Angelier. Will that be the way? Don't you think it will be long enough without my fourth name of Hamilton?

—M.M.H.L.

Madeleine wrote Emile again on the eve of his departure for Badgemore.

My Own Dear Emile,

I must bid you adieu in this note. May you enjoy your trip, be happy with your friends, and may you again return in health, safety, and happiness to Glasgow.

I do wonder if you are in Helensburgh tonight. I fancy no—something says you are not.

I had an invitation yesterday from some friends in London to go and pay them a visit—not Bessie—but Mama would not allow me. So I have declined, for which I am very sorry.

We are to have friends from Ireland next week, among the number a very nice young fellow with a large mustache. If you wish to cut all the hair off your face, why then do it, but I am sure it won't improve your appearance in the least.

A letter sent to Emile at the end of September, after his uneventful trip to Badgemore, indicated that her father's repeated invitations to William Minnoch were continuing to cause Madeleine to view the quiet businessman in a different light—which was James Smith's plan from the start.

MY OWN EVER DEAR EMILE,

I did not write you Sunday—as Christina was not at home, so I could not get it posted.

I don't think I can see you this week—but I think next Monday night I shall, as Papa and Mama are to be in Edinburgh. But my only thought is Janet—what am I to do with her? I shall have to wait till she is asleep, which may be near eleven o'clock. But you may be sure I shall do it as soon as I can. I expect great pleasure at seeing you.

As a favor, do not refer to what is past.

Mr. Minnoch has been here since Friday. He is most agreeable. We shall see him very often this winter—he says we shall—and Papa being so fond of him, I am sure he shall ask him in often.

There is a chance I may be in Glasgow tomorrow, but I am not sure till I see Papa tonight. But Bessie will be with me, and I would not see you. I may not go, but I think we shall. There is a chance of our being in Glasgow the end of October.

Papa is not well, and he finds it too much going up and down from Glasgow to Row.

But I can write no more at present—so with very kind much love,

your ever dear
MIMI.

P.S. I have just got word of the death of my old sweetheart in Edinburgh—for which I am not in the least sorry. Love again to you, sweet one.

Her postscript is startling in its harshness. Unless the dead man had treated her badly, it is hard to comprehend her callous view of his demise. Her coldness was not meant to pacify Emile's jealousy, because she would not have mentioned the dead man at all if that had been her goal, nor would she have referred to Minnoch in such a flattering light.

Emile did not like Madeleine's easing acceptance of Minnoch into the inner circle of the Smith home, and he rebuked her during a visit to Rowaleyn in early October, even questioning his love for her. In a letter dated the following morning (with a postscript added later as a weak attempt to soften the letter's impact), Madeleine gave Emile a rare and honest glimpse of her own psyche, and for the first time pondered the incompatibility of their "marriage."

MY DEAR EMILE,

The day is cold, so I shall not go out. So I shall spend a little time in writing you.

Our meeting last night was peculiar. Emile, you are not reasonable. I do not wonder at your not loving me as you once did . . . I see misery before me this winter.

I would to God we were not to be so near Mr. Minnoch—you shall hear all stories and believe them. You will say I am indifferent because I shall not be able to see you much.

I could not sleep all night. I thought of your unhappy appearance. You shed tears, love—but I did not. Yes, you must think me cool. But it is my nature.

Emile, my sweet darling, love causes unhappiness in more ways than one. I know you will—I feel sure you will—quarrel with me this winter. I know it well, sweet love. But God only knows, dearest, that I have no desire ever to be parted from you. So, Emile, if we should ever part it will be on your side—not mine.

I sometimes fancy you are disappointed with me. I am not what you once thought I was. I am too much of a child to please you. I am too fond of amusement to suit your fancy. I am too indifferent, and I do not mind what the world says—not in the least—I never did.

I trust we have days of happiness before us—but God knows we have days of misery, too.

Emile, my own, my ever dear husband, I have suffered much on your account from my family. They have laughed at my love for you—they taunted me regarding you. I was watched all last winter. I was not allowed out by myself for fear I should meet you. But if I can, I shall cheat them this winter. I shall avoid you at first, and that may cause them to allow me out by myself. I shall write you as often as I can, but it cannot be the three times a week it has been.

I shall never forget last night.

There is a sentence still in my ear: you said about "God striking you dead" if ever you meet me again. Since my childhood, that is a sentence I have shuddered to hear expressed. When I was very young, about five years old, a woman made use of that sentence on my Grandpapa's farm—and she was struck dead that hour. It has never left me since. I heard you say it.

I have come to the conclusion that you do not know me. If you were with me long, you would know me better. It is only those I love that I am indifferent to. Even my dog, which I love—sometimes I hate it, and for no reason. It is only a fancy which I cannot help. To strangers it is different. I do love you truly and fondly.

Do you still wish to show your [portrait] to a [female] friend?

I hope I did not show much temper to you last night—did I, sweet love?

Adieu for the present. I am thy ever true and ever loving and dear,
MIMI L'ANGELIER.

[*the next morning*]

P.S. My own dear little pet—I hope you are well. Mama and Papa got home last night. I don't know if I should send you the note I wrote yesterday. If you don't like it—burn it. I hope to have a letter from you some day next week—send it by way of Christina.

We are quite full of company. Saturday and Monday we are to have a large dinner party. I shall tell you in my next letter the way I think we shall do your letters in the coming winter [at the new house]. Adieu, dear love.

If Emile did reply to this letter, Madeleine makes no mention of it in her next letter, written late in the evening on Sunday, October 20. By this time, Emile had moved into the Franklin Place lodging house kept by Mrs. Ann Jenkins.

MY VERY DEAR EMILE,

This has been a long, wet, nasty day. I would have given the world if you had been here to talk to me. I have been so stupid it would only have been you that could have made me feel alive.

I think we shall leave Row for Glasgow in three weeks—that is, if the house shall be ready for us.

Papa is very busy with some matters connecting the coming elections—so we won't be able to go to Bridge of Allan.

James is liking school very much—only, poor boy, he complains of not getting enough sugar or butter. Fancy, he pays £80 for his board alone—it is far too much for such a boy, is it not?

Janet is not well, she has a dreadful bad cold.

Do you know I have taken a great dislike to Christina [Haggart]? I shall try and do without her aid in the winter. She has been with us four years, and I am tired of her. But I won't show it to her, so be easy on that point.

I know who it was that saw me walking to Helensburgh and told you—it was the Kennedys. A few minutes before I saw them I had been jumping and running with my large Newfoundland dog, Major, and when I saw it was them, I thanked my stars I was just walking. Their brother was with them—I did not know them. Bessie knew them, and told me it was them.

Papa has sold his horse, and the one he has got he is not going to bring down here this season. I am to have a pony to myself next summer. I told a horse jockey man to look out for one yesterday. I think Papa means to drive a pair next summer. Anything for a little more expense.

So you still like your lodgings? If you are not coming on the Sunday night, but on Saturday, that is fine. Remember, you are to come on whichever night suits you.

[*P.S. the next morning*]

I am just going off to Dumbarton. The carriage will be here in ten minutes, and I am to have breakfast before I go. I am just up—it's half past ten—you are horrified.

The "marriage" was starting to come undone. Madeleine's plans involving the pony clearly indicate her belief that she would be back at Row the following summer, and not living with Emile in a newlywed house.

The Smith family journeyed back to Glasgow for the winter and settled into their "town" life in their new home on Blythswood Square. Madeleine and Janet shared a room below street level, with windows opening onto the street. Her first letter to Emile from the new house is dated November 18, 1856.

MY OWN SWEET DARLING,

I am at home all safe—and very well.

I do assure you it was with no small pleasure I received your note today. It is such a time since I have heard from you. But we must so contrive that I shall hear from you every week. But I must see all about it first—and shall let you know as soon as I can. Though I think it is a great piece of self-denial not to meet each other. I should so much like to see you. Do you not think I could sometimes see you at a window of a Sunday, and no one would know of it? I would see you, love, and that would be enough.

I don't like this house—it is not at all to my mind.

Though Papa did not look ill, yet he was ill.

Could you believe it—I walked eight miles yesterday and did not feel tired.

You are a naughty boy to go and dream of me.

I shall tell you in my next note of a poor young fellow at Stirling who has fallen in love with your Mimi. But don't fear—it is not returned. I am sorry for him.

Soon after her arrival back in Glasgow, Madeleine fulfilled the promise of getting her ambrotype portrait made for Emile. In a letter written just after her posing session, she related the experience: "I know you won't look on my likeness with pleasure—it is so cross—but, love, when it was done, I had been in the horrid man's place from twelve o'clock, and I had it closed at four o'clock. I had had no food since the night before, and I was very furious."

The remainder of her letter told Emile the latest news and hearsay:

Did you go to the concert? I did. Jack went—he came in, had ordered the cab, and brought me my gloves. He always does that when I am going out with him. So I went, and Bessie. I looked at everyone, but could not see my husband. Mr. Minnoch was there with his horrid old sister—but I only bowed to them. I have not seen any of them yet. I don't understand why Papa has not asked him to dinner yet.

There is rather a coolness with us and the aunts this season. We shall not see them much. We have only seen them once.

Sweet love, you should get those brown envelopes—they would not be so much seen as the white ones put down into my window. You should stoop down to tie your shoe, and then slip it in.

The back door is closed. Mama keeps the key for fear our servant boy would go out of an evening. We have got blinds for our windows.

When you write William [Stevenson, Emile's friend and supervisor at Huggins and Company], give him my very kind love. I should so much like to know the kind friend of my dear husband. Tell him how glad I shall be to become friends with him. I saw Robert Anderson the other day—he was speaking of Huggins—but he did not speak of you. He fancies I am going to take Mr. Minnoch.

I am sure you won't like me in my jacket. I don't like it—both Papa and Mama do. My bonnet is fawn. Bessie has a pink one, and Mama wanted me to have pink—but I knew you would think pink very vulgar. Dear love, when I am your wife, I shall require you to tell me what I am to wear—as I have no idea of dress myself. Mama and Bessie do all that for me. My dress this winter is to be dark gray tweed—you will like that, I am sure.

Emile, I shall tell you in confidence that I don't think we shall ever live at Row again. Papa is going to look at some property on Monday near Edinburgh, and if he can get a nice large place, Row will be sold. But he won't sell it till he gets another.

I have been ordered by the doctor since I came to town to take a fearful thing called "piece meal." Such a nasty thing. I am to take it at luncheon. But I don't think I can take this meal. I shall rather take cocoa.

One has to wonder, considering Emile's jealousy, why Madeleine mentioned William Minnoch so often in her letters written during the winter of 1856–57. Two theories have been put forth by her biographers:

- Madeleine felt that it would be better to tell Emile of her interaction with Minnoch herself, rather than for Emile to find out later from some other source and then exaggerate the situation or accuse her of secrecy. She wanted to tell him the story first, in the way she wanted him to believe it.
- Madeleine enjoyed Emile's jealous tantrums.

The truth may be either, or may lie somewhere between the two.

Her portrait completed, Madeleine sent it to Emile by way of Christina Haggart and enclosed a penciled note:

BELOVED EMILE,

I hope you will have this tonight. Accept it with my best, my kindest love. A kiss, sweet darling—I don't know if you shall have a letter from me again before Monday, but I shall try.

I was at the concert—Mama was with me, and Jack and Bessie.

I have put up this likeness in an old book so that it may not be felt to be glass.

I am just going out.

> Ever thine, thy own fond wife,
> thy MIMI.

Madeleine was apparently the only member of the Smith household who disliked the new Blythswood Square residence, and her aversion seemingly spread to all of Glasgow: "I feel quite ill in this horrid place—Glasgow. I hate it so. I never thought the people looked so vulgar as they do now. They are a most vulgar-looking set. I wish I were out of this horrid town—what a place it is—I would not like to spend my life in such a place."

The layout of the new house was not as favorable for actual face-to-face meetings as the India Street residence had been, and even whispered conversations at her bedroom window were more challenging, due in part to the constant nightly presence of her sister Janet. While formulating new plans for their rendezvous, Madeleine quickly devised new strategies for the exchange of their letters:

> I wish you to write me and give me the note on Tuesday evening next. You will . . . come and put the letter down into the window. Mine is the window next to Minnoch's door. There are two windows together with white blinds. Don't be seen near the house on Sunday, as Mama won't be at church, and she will watch. . . . [If] it is more convenient for you to drop in my note at six o'clock—do it . . . if not at six, why, I shall look at eight. I hope no one sees you, darling—make no noise at the window.

In her next letter, she referred to William Minnoch by a nickname that would surely inflame Emile's jealousy ("Drop the note in between the bars . . . [at] the window with a white blind next to Billy's door"), and then went on to describe the "poor young fellow at Stirling" she had mentioned in a previous letter.

> I was to tell you about the poor young fellow at Stirling. Well he, poor, stupid boy, would keep so near me—and only speak to me—and to finish all, he told me he could only ever love me. I told him I did not care a bit for him—and, fancy, he began to weep. I was near weeping too—for I feel so sorry always to see a man shed tears. After a little, I told him he was very foolish, and that he was never to think of me again. The day we came home, he rode for about six miles after our carriage—and then returned. But I expect he will be coming to call one of these days soon. I promised him I would not tell any of my family, as they would laugh at him so. You are the only one I would tell. Is it not fun?

Similar to the episodes involving Minnoch, it is puzzling why Madeleine divulged the story of this young gentleman. She may have wanted to illustrate her undying devotion to Emile by her complete rejection of the suitor, but it would have been far safer never to mention other gentlemen who paid respects to her.

She began her next letter with a reference to her portrait, which Emile had not yet mentioned receiving.

> I cannot resist the temptation of writing you a line this evening.
>
> By this time, you have my parcel. I hope ere long you may have the original, which I know you will like better than a glass likeness—won't you, sweet love? I hope you got it safe—Christina left it at the door for you.

I intend going—if the day is fine—to Row on Saturday with Papa. It may be the last time I may ever be there. But I don't care, so as I end up with you, love.

You were annoyed at Minnoch going to the concert with me—I know I was, for I knew it would vex *you*, but all this annoyance will soon end—so don't vex yourself about it.

I am glad you promised not to say anything to Minnoch. And you will ask no one to speak to him for you. You know, dear, it would all come back on your wife—so I know, sweet love, you won't annoy him.

I did read [Harriet Beecher Stowe's] "Dred," but was disgusted with it. It was one wet Sunday at Row, and I had nothing to do, so I read the whole of it.

Emile, I don't see when we are to have a chance for our marriage. I don't know, but I rather think Papa and Mama will go into Edinburgh with James in January, but I don't hear of their being from home in February. How I am to get out of the house in the morning with my things—which will be two large boxes, etc.—I don't know. I rather think they might go the night before. And for that, I would try and get the back door key. The banns give me great fright. I wish there was any way to get quit of them. What stupid things they are. I don't see the use of them—do you, sweet darling?

I called for the Tweedies today, but I knew they always go out at two o'clock—so we called at three o'clock, and, as I expected, they were "not at home." For which I was very glad. They asked us four times last winter—which we never went, and never did we ask them.

We met several gentlemen in town today who asked to have the pleasure of dancing with us at Thomson's Ball tonight. But I said we did not intend to go to any Glasgow Balls this winter. I shall just laugh at the aunts the next time they speak of that report!

Is it the MacDougals in Elembank Crescent that you mean are such gossips? One of them always laughs when she sees me—it is a pretty one, with light hair. Jack admires her so and thinks there is no girl in town like her. You used to think so, too.

I see [Monsieur] de Mean passing our house. How is Madame? Have you been to see them yet? I would not like to live with my relations as they do. I would rather have a small place and be with my husband only. I don't like friends in the house. We shall often talk over all our past performances—it really has been quite a small romance.

How things do come about! Did you or I fancy, that first morning we met in Sauchiehall Street, that we should yet be husband and wife? I am sure I never did! What were my feelings that morning? I thought you would think me bold and impudent coming out to meet you, a stranger. I wept for an hour after I got home for having done such a thing. I thank God now I did it, or we would not have been as we are, my love, my husband.

My dear, if I was to take, as you say, a glass of port wine, I would *not* be unable to stand. Two spoonfuls of port is enough for me, however. But don't fear, I am very strong and can stand a very great deal.

> I am your own, your fond wife,
> MIMI L'ANGELIER.

P.S. Please tell me, love, what that "P" before Emile stands for—I must know all your names.

Another letter was posted a few days later, and touched on a variety of subjects, beginning with Madeleine's health ("I did not go to Row—I had a bad headache when I woke at six o'clock, so I thought it best not to go, in case of cold."), continuing with the comings and goings of her siblings ("Jack has just come home from Edinburgh . . . James dined with him tonight—he is to be home on Friday. Janet is a good girl, but she is not very affectionate . . . "), and concluding with reports of her good behavior:

> I am doing all I can to be good. Considering the way we walked every other winter, I am behaving very well. But, sweet Emile, you don't think so. I fancy I see by your look. Everyone is asking why Bessie and I are not walking on Sauchiehall Street in the afternoons. Mama was quite annoyed we did not go out several times this week. You don't mind when Mama is with us, do you? When we go out with her, she always comes home by Sauchiehall. . . .

In the midst of this lengthy letter, Madeleine focused once again on their future wedding, suggesting that a Justice of the Peace perform the ceremony, in order to avoid the dreaded banns. She reported that Christina Haggart had agreed to send her belongings ahead to wherever the secret wedding would take place.

In a somewhat darker mood, Madeleine also wondered about her feelings for their future children: "Emile, I would like to have a child, because I know you are fond of children. Only I would be very jealous of the baby, as I would not then get so much of your love. I would envy every loving word or look you bestowed on the child."

Miss Mary Perry came back into the story during the early winter of 1856, when she announced that she could not continue writing to Madeleine if Mrs. Smith did not know of the correspondence. This information was relayed to

Madeleine by Emile. Madeleine was furious, lashing out in her next letter at Miss Perry and knowingly attacking Emile at his weakest point:

> Why did Miss Perry not find out at first that it was wrong to write me? It looks as if she had taken some dislike to me. But I shall never write her again since she thinks it so very wrong. It is a pity she has written to me at all [in the past]. It has vexed me a good deal. Even you do not say a word on the subject, dear Emile.
>
> Dear me, dear Emile. Have you only £50 [per year] from Huggins? I thought you had £100. How could I make such a mistake? I wonder you stay for such a small sum. You could have much more. . . .

Emile took a short vacation soon after his receipt of this letter, and Madeleine's next correspondence went to his holiday address. Tensions appeared to have calmed between the two, but Madeleine still spent much of her next letter retracting the contents of her previous one—and once again defending herself for speaking to a man at a social event.

> I am so glad that you are enjoying yourself. I do like to hear that you are happy and well. I am so glad that you have met so much nice company. Do you not, sweet love, forget your Mimi when you are among all these young ladies? Do you never wish you were free to love another? But it is not fair of me to speak to you so—you are so good, so kind, so loving.
>
> You have misunderstood me regarding your income. What I meant when I said about the £50, was that I did think it was much too little for you to receive for your services. You told me you had £100, and I was satisfied with the sum—and I tell you again it is quite enough. Yes, it is enough. I am satisfied with the sum—it is enough for all our wants. We, I trust, have many years of happiness before us—years that we shall enjoy our life, and meet with no disappointments nor annoyances.
>
> I was sorry I said anything about Mary—it was not kind of me. She is your kind and true friend—but I was vexed she said she would not write me. I thought she had taken some dislike to me and would not write me. She had written me all along knowing Mama did not know—so I thought it peculiar she should drop writing without such other excuse. Pray, love, do not say a word to her about my writing in an unkind way. She is your friend, and that is enough. She shall be mine some day soon—she won't object then, shall she?
>
> Sweet dear, I could not help being introduced to Sir Chamberland. I met him up at the Wilsons. I did not know he was there—but I don't like him in the least. I hope never to see him again—don't be angry, love. I could not help it—pray pardon me, dear love.

Good-bye for the present. Ever yours,
MIMI L'ANGELIER.

P.S. If I had wings, I would be with you this night. Good night. A kiss.

December of 1856 opened with a letter from Madeleine full of regrets for causing Emile's unhappiness, apologies for being seen in public with her own brother ("I shall avoid going out with Jack as much as I can—he is in Edinburgh—will that, love, please you?"), and questions about Emile's impending visitor, *D. E.*—whom Emile apparently wished to avoid.

> You are in a fix with D. E. What can you do? Will you ask him to come? Is there no more spare room in your lodging for him? When he proposes, you cannot well refuse.

> And, dear love, will you go abroad with him next summer? Will I not be your wife by that time? We could not part so soon, dearest pet. I will be very unfond of being left alone. Of course, if it is business, then I would not say a word. I should not like to be left alone in bed—it would be so cold, so dull.

> I am not going out on Wednesday night. I have an invitation for Edinburgh in February. I have written to say I will give no answer about it till the time comes—and we shall see.

> But I had an invitation yesterday which will make you laugh. Where do you think it was to? New York! I had told some friends in London I would much like to go, and they are going in April, so they said if I was still in the same mind, would I go with them? It was all fun on my part. When I heard of it, love, I was sure you would have a good laugh.

> I have told you, I think, that I have nothing to do with housekeeping now. I gave it up when we left Row, [but] Mama says I must take it up again in summer. [I'm not now required] to go out and make markets. I like to do it very much in the country, but not in town. Mama is tired of it, but I won't take it off her hands.

> You mistake me. The snobs I spoke of do not know anything of me. They see a light [in my bedroom basement window] and they fancy it may be the servant's room—and they may have some fun. Only you know I sleep downstairs. I never told anyone, so don't knock again, my beloved.

Fearful of someone in the house looking out and seeing him, Madeleine often warned Emile not to make any noise when leaving a letter for her.

The winter holidays approached and William Minnoch became a more frequent guest in the Smith household. Minnoch became much clearer concerning his intentions toward Madeleine, and she easily foresaw an approaching marriage proposal. This increase in Minnoch's presence did not go unnoticed by Emile, and the Glasgow merchant became the topic of repeated quarrels and rebukes, leaving Madeleine to defend herself as best she could.

It was Minnoch that I was at the concert with. You see: I would not hide that from you. Emile, he is Papa's friend, and I know he will have him at the house. But need you mind that? When I have told you I have no regard for him? It is only you, my Emile, that I love. You should not mind public report. You know I am your wife, and that we shall shortly be united—so, Emile, it matters not. I promised you I should be seen as little in public with him as I could. I have avoided him at all times. But, I could not on Wednesday night—so, sweet love, be reasonable. I love you. Is not that enough?

Beginning in December of 1856, Madeleine's letters made frequent mention of Emile's former loves, including the "Lady from Fife," and spoke often of how unworthy she was to be his wife—an effort, perhaps, to direct his affections elsewhere. It was a thread her letters would carry through to the end.

My Own Beloved Darling,

I am longing for Thursday to bring me your dear, sweet letter.

I was wrong about a clergyman being able to marry without banns—it seems he cannot. I asked our own clergyman today, Mr. Middleton. I asked it as a passing remark.

I am going to the concert tomorrow. It is the last one. I do not know if Minnoch is going—I have not heard.

James and Janet have sent out nearly fifty invitations today for their party on [December] the 29th. James is to be home on Friday. Last evening we had a good many young friends.

I would give anything to have an hour's chat with you. But, beloved Emile, I don't see how we can. Mama is not going from home, and when Papa is away, Janet does not sleep with Mama, as she used to do. She won't leave me, as I have a fire in my room, and Mama has none. Do you think, beloved, you could not see me some night for a few minutes at the door under the front door? But perhaps it would not be safe. Someone might pass as you were coming in. We had better not. But I would so like a kiss, dear—and I think I could also say you would like one from your Mimi. Am I right?

Miss Wilson is going to take Sir H. C. after all. She is to be married the second week in February in your church, St. Jude. They have come to stay in town. Sir Henry is with them. I am to be in town tomorrow.

Is not this nasty weather?

Did [Monsieur] de Mean go to Helensburgh on Saturday? His wife was not with him. Can they part so soon? I hope we won't be without each other for as much as a night for a long, long time. I heard Madame de Mean was at the concert in the McLelland Rooms—and looked very well.

By the by, darling, do you still admire Laura Kerr? I hear her Mama has someone in view for her at present.

What little "white fib" did you tell D. E.? Have you written Willmers yet? I hope you have. I quite liked him from his style of letter and his affection for my own beloved husband. And his sister is a nice girl, I am sure.

I often wonder, knowing all the nice girls you know, why you should have fixed upon me as you did. I often wonder: what your other young lady, the one that disappointed you, was like. Was she pretty? Am I anything like her? I shall get you to tell me all the girls you have loved. And then I shall begin, when you tell me of pretty ones, to be very jealous.

You may flirt as much as you like after our marriage, for I know you love me, so I have all confidence.

Many of her biographers note a marked shift in tone in Madeleine's final letters of 1856. These letters, and those that followed in the first three months of 1857, are briefer and the tone is more anxious. Emile noticed this and Madeleine responded:

I cannot give you any reason for my letters being short. I have no reason. Oh, if I were just with you and all this annoyance past, it would make me feel as if I had heart to do things. But at present I see things not improving one bit. I see no chance for us. I never felt so disheartened as I do now, for I see nothing bright for the future. . . .

Madeleine would spend much of the remaining correspondence denying the rumors about herself and Minnoch that had filtered down to Emile—and he challenged her on each one.

My Beloved, My Darling,

Do you for a moment think I could feel happy this evening, knowing you were in low spirits—and that I am the cause? Oh, why was I ever born to annoy you? Do you not wish—oh yes, full well I know you often wish—you had never known me?

You say you heard that I took Minnoch to the concert against his inclination—I forced him to go. I told you the right way it happened when I wrote. But from your statement in your letter of tonight, you did not believe my word. Emile, I would not have done this to you. Every word you write or tell me I would believe. I would not believe every idle report. No, I would not. But you always listen to reports about me if they are bad. I know I talked with him. I could not sit there a whole evening without talking—but I did not flirt. I gave up flirting some time ago. There is a difference between flirting and talking. Minnoch was not with me last night—he had some second-rate looking girl with him of the name of Christie. John MacKenzie was engaged to her for two years.

Darling, do not think of dark clouds—they may pass away, and all will be sunshine. Emile, you do not look on the bright side of the picture. I do—[because] I cannot look on the dark. Do not give way to such sad, dark thoughts. All will end well.

For your sake I shall be very kind to Janet. Her party is spoiled—as all the people James has asked are grown-up ladies and gentlemen. He has asked the Tweedies! He has asked who he would like, and he sent through a list.

I hate our houseboy, William. He stands out on the street every night, and we are very angry with him. I give him a blow up every day. I just gave him your note along with four others and said nothing. We have a nasty cook, too. I am rather more fond of Christina now—she is very civil. I would trust her. But I shall always take in my own notes, love—that will please you.

Emile, my beloved, I would love your child—could I help it? I would be to it a fond mother. I would forget the suffering, knowing it was a pledge of our love. Thank you for saying you would love me more if I had a child, and that I need not be jealous. I would rather a son, as he might have a greater chance of being like his father. And when you were away from me, I should have him to look at.

Emile, darling, I think I can promise that I shall not be out on the streets on Saturday. I shall go out in the forenoon, come in about 1:30, and not go out again. It will please you if I do so—so I shall do it, sweet love.

I did not see you on Monday. Bessie said nothing. She never, by any chance, mentions your name to me. I heard her ask Aunt if you were in Glasgow, as she had not seen you. Bessie said she did not think Madeleine had *ever* seen you [this season]!

Mama has been very ill all day and in bed. She is very ill tonight. Papa has come home—he could not stay away, she is so ill.

Tell me what Mary says of my likeness. It is horrid ugly.

You say Miss Willmers asks you in her last letter for a description of your wife? I would give a great deal to see your account of little Mimi. It will be like this: a short, fat, round-faced thing. Give me a copy of your account.

Christmas Day of 1856 did not in any way foreshadow the tumultuous events that would occur in the three months that followed.

MY VERY DEAR EMILE,

I hope you are well this night.

I have never felt so tired as I am of Christmas Day. We have had a large dinner party—all old people. I have wished, I am sure, a thousand times I had been by your side in your own little room.

Christmas Eve we had a few friends. Minnoch was with us—he is to be with us on Monday evening, and also on the last night of the year.

I have a very severe headache this night. I am not able to write much.

Poor Janet was very ill this morning. She had danced so much—she is a very good dancer—last evening from seven o'clock till one o'clock, that when she got up this morning, she fainted. I did get a fright with her. I thought the child was dead. She is not at all well tonight. She is out tomorrow night again.

James is very much subdued—but improved in appearance.

My own dear Emile, were you at chapel today? I intended to have been at the Roman Catholic Church today, but I was prevented from going.

My last letters to you must have seemed unkind—pray, my love, forgive me.

Beloved Emile, we must meet. If you love me, you will come to me when Papa and Mama are away in Edinburgh—which I think will be the 7th or 10th of January. Love, we must meet. Do not disappoint me, sweet love.

I shall take your hint and give it to Bessie about the Tweedies. I don't like the family at all, and I shall never be intimate with them. They are coming to our house on an invitation sent to them in Janet and James's names, and they sent back their answer addressed to James alone. Papa hates their father, and would not have him come to the house. I don't know him.

I shall do all I can to learn painting—and soon.

My beloved Emile, I did not go out on Saturday after one o'clock in the afternoon. Bessie and Jack took a walk in Sauchiehall Street at three o'clock by themselves. Are you pleased, beloved one of my soul?

My letter of Friday must have gone amissing. It has no return address, so it won't come back here again.

Mama is rather better—it was influenza she had. James and Janet go out every night this week after Tuesday—to the Rowans on Wednesday. I hate Christmas dinners, etc.—they are such a bore.

Our rooms are very small, and there are fifty people coming. That impudent-looking fellow Banks is to play for us. You remember—he was in the Exhibition.

Will you give me a letter on Friday at six o'clock? I say six because I have promised, if I can, to go with Jack to the Pantomime. Papa is at Row on that night, and Bessie and I and Jack intend going. If not at six o'clock, why then, if you like, at ten o'clock.

I must stop asking your forgiveness for my unkindness. Forgive me, your wife, your own Mimi, asking you forgiveness. Smile upon me.

I need not wish you a merry Xmas, but I shall wish that we may spend the next together, and that we shall then be happy.

> Adieu, my dear Emile. Believe me, thine ever true, devoted,
>   affectionate wife,
>   MIMI L'ANGELIER.

Minnoch had been a frequent guest of the Smith family over the Christmas holidays, and the family presumed that he would propose marriage in the near future. Madeleine was at a loss for how to proceed. Her last letter of 1856 was a long and rambling one.

MY OWN EVER BELOVED EMILE,

Thank you, sweet one, for your assurance of your love. I love you.

But, Emile, I feel sad tonight, and why I cannot tell. If I were with you I would be all right. But I feel ready to weep and sigh.

Sweet pet, I know your love for me is great when I am good—but you are cool when I am bad, and then I try to drown my sad thoughts in being careless. When I get a cool letter from you, my beloved, I feel as if I did not care what I did or where I went.

I know the walks you propose—they are good ones.

It is a pity they have not written for you to come home [to Jersey]—it might do you good—change of air and company.

Mama is better.

I did not much like the Pantomime. It was stupid, but I suppose it is as good as a Pantomime can be. Jack and Bessie and I and a friend of Jack's named Patison went.

Why, you little pet, you were in Bath Street when I saw you Tuesday. I passed you quite close. It was you—it must have been Emile L'Angelier. I did not make a mistake.

I have not yet got consent about the painting lessons, but I don't fear.

I think I shall have to go to Edinburgh in the beginning of February. They are so anxious to have us. I have again refused to stay at the Castle. Even Bessie says she would not like to go.

I don't understand why you did not get a note from me on Thursday—it was posted at eleven o'clock—time enough for you to get it at three o'clock.

Give my love to Mary. I thought she did not "know" me. I am so glad she is your dear friend. I wish I had one like her—it would do me a vast deal of good.

Now, I must tell you something you may hear. I was at the Theatre, and people, my love, may tell you that Minnoch was there too. Well, love, he was there, but he did not know of my going. He was in the Club Box, and I did not even bow to him. Today, when Bessie, Mama, and I were walking, Minnoch joined us, took a walk with us, and came home—he was most civil and kind. He sent Janet such a lovely flower tonight to wear on Monday evening.

Now I have told you this, sweet pet. I know you will be angry, but I would rather bear your anger than that you would perhaps blame me for not telling you—as someone will be sure to inform you of me. I have been candid with you, as I think it is best—is it not, my sweet one?

I often think if I were to displease you and you were to go away—what would I do? I would get someone to take me to be their wife, but I would never love another one. I have no love for any other but you, my sweet Emile. I often fear you will yet get so cool to me that you won't have me for your wife. For, however much I adore you—if you were cool, I would not be your wife.

What are you to do on New Year's Day? It is always a horrid day to me. I never go out, and we have such a host of people to call for us—all coming in, making such a fuss, wishing happy returns, etc. It is a great bore.

I have not read your book regarding Sir J. Franklin. We have not got it—but I know someone who has. But I don't think you would like me to ask the lend of it from Minnoch.

My dear Emile, I must say adieu. Your ever true and devoted,
MIMI L'ANGELIER.

P.S. How bad Robert Baird is behaving! They sometimes throw out a hint at your being one of his friends. He introduced me to you. I shall always feel a warm heart towards him. Good night, beloved.

It is interesting to note her statement: "I would get someone to take me to be their wife," when she had previously maintained that she could not or would not marry another. This change of heart may have been an initial attempt to force Emile into considering the possibility of her marrying another, or it could merely indicate the vacillating state of her troubled mind. Either way, her feelings and thoughts regarding Emile had changed, and would continue to do so.

Madeleine knew she could not refuse a marriage proposal from William Minnoch. Her family would never accept the impoverished Emile as a reason for not marrying an upstanding businessman. In a late 1856 letter to Mary Perry, with whom things had been patched up, Madeleine began to set the foundation for the upcoming separation ("No one in this world escapes sorrow, and [Emile], like the rest, must submit"), while simultaneously maintaining that she and Emile would soon be husband and wife.

Part V

The 1857 Correspondence

MADELEINE'S FIRST LETTER TO EMILE in the new year, dated January 9, 1857, followed a hushed conversation at her bedroom window. Emile had recently injured his hand to the extent that he could not write to her. Although she fully knew the reason for his inability to correspond, Emile's silence, as usual, agitated Madeleine.

> It is just eleven o'clock and no letter from you, my own very dear husband. Why this, my sweet one? I think I heard your stick this evening—pray, do not make any sounds whatever at my window. I fear your finger is bad. If it were possible, sweet one, could you not leave my notes at six, as at ten—as the moon is up and it is light?
>
> I was so glad to see you the other night. When we shall meet again, I cannot tell. I hope you have gone and seen Mary, and also that you have made up your mind to go to Edinburgh and see your kind, dear friends, the Lanes. Are they to be long in Scotland?
>
> By the by, did I [mistakenly] put a letter [in with] yours addressed to Clara Courtland? If I did not, I have put it into some other letter. I found the envelope addressed, but no note could I get—so if you have got hold of it, just put it into the fire, as I have written another one.
>
> We are going to a large Ball at the Wilsons' on the third of February.
>
> Is not this horrid bad weather? I have been very little out all week—it is so cold. How do you keep warm in bed—for I have a fire and Janet—and I am not a bit warm.

I often wish I could take a peep into the future. If I could see what would be in two or three years hence. But perhaps it would be bad for us if we knew what would happen.

I am writing in the Dining Room—and I think you are again at my window. But I shall not go downstairs, as Papa would wonder why, and only he and I are up waiting for Jack.

Do you, sweet, beloved Emile, still like your lodgings? Are they comfortable, and are the people kind to you? Have you gone to any doctor yet—or are you still being doctor yourself, my own best beloved?

Adieu. A kiss, my pet, my sweet one.
MIMI L'ANGELIER

P.S. Why did you not write me tonight, my pet, my love? But your hand is bad, I know it is.

Do you hear of Louise now, or is she still in country?

I am so sorry to think your hand may be very bad, and you have no one to dress you or do anything for you. If I were beside you, I would do everything for you: dress you, wash your face—but I fear I could not shave you. I tried to do it for Jack in the summer and cut him—but do you shave or not?

I hope you may get this tomorrow. It shall be posted long before twelve o'clock, so it won't be my fault. I don't understand the post.

Madeleine's attempts to balance Emile and Minnoch became more strained as January continued. She hinted at the problem in her next letter: "My sweet, dear pet, I would so like to spend three or four hours with you, just to talk over some things, but I do not know when we can."

Emile's hand healed and he replied to her recent letters. As she had suspected, she had inadvertently enclosed a letter to her friend, Clara Courtland, in the same envelope with a letter to Emile—but instead of destroying it, as she requested, Emile had read it and questioned her on its contents.

MY OWN BELOVED DARLING HUSBAND,

I have written Mary a note, and you shall have one too.

I shall contrive to see you some night soon for a short time. I do not know when they may go from home. I wish I could tell you—but I don't see any chance, as Mama is not well this winter. It would be difficult to get away from cousin's house in Edinburgh, but I do so wish we could be married.

In my letter to Clara I said that about seeing her in the summer for politeness sake. I know there is no chance, as she goes to India in June to get married. She is an officer's daughter. Her father was in the same regiment with two of Papa's brothers.

The man Patison, Jack's friend, is not from Ayr—he was born in America. You must know his father, as he does business with America. Godfrey Patison—he is just nineteen, but Bessie has a great fancy for him, so he is much with us. He is a nice boy. Grierson is a most innocent fellow.

I will stop for tonight.

P.S. [the next evening] It is very late, and I am too tired to write, so you will excuse me.

I think you should leave the office for some time, and go and get a change of air—it would be good for you.

Mr. Kirk has been here today, and we have fixed to go to Edinburgh at the end of February. He wishes us to go to several Balls. I think we shall go to one Ball in Glasgow. I don't hear of Mama or Papa going from home, so, my dear pet, I see no chance for us. I fear we shall have to wait a bit. I don't see how I could venture to [get married] while in Edinburgh, but if I see or hear anything—you shall hear of it.

Mr. Minnoch dined with us tonight. Do you know, I think if you knew him you would like him—he is most kind. I like him very much better than I used to do.

I hope, dear love, you will be soon better. I am engaged every night this week. I have sent a note to Mary—don't give it [to her] if you don't like it.

This letter clearly shows Madeleine's clumsy attempts to control the approaching dilemma. She suggests that Emile leave town, probably so that he would not hear of her formal engagement to Minnoch, and attempts to convince Emile that the man who would soon become her other fiancé was a fine person whose company Emile would enjoy. The threads of the web were drawing tighter around her.

Soon after the previous letter, Madeleine and Emile passed each other on the street. It was not a pleasant episode, and Madeleine wrote later:

Well, my dear Emile, you did look cross at your Mimi the other day. Why, my pet, you cannot expect I am never to go on St. Vincent Street. Sometimes I must. It is not quite fair of you. I have kept off that street so well this winter, and yet when you meet me, and the first time you have bowed to me this season, that you should have looked so cross! When I saw you coming, I felt frightened even to bow to you.

Later in the same letter, she once again pointed Emile directly toward another of his admirers and encouraged him to enhance his social life.

Have you written to Miss Williams? "No," I can hear you say. Well, you naughty boy, when she was so kind to write to you, why not do it?

I hope you will enjoy your trip to Edinburgh. You will—when you are among all your dear friends. Do, my dear Emile, go to the officers' Ball. It will do you good to get a little excitement. You need not dance much—but go, sweet one.

Her next letter followed a late-night visit from Emile, where the couple once again talked quietly through her open bedroom window—young Janet being asleep in the same room. She ended the letter: "I don't think I should send you this scroll, but I could not help it: just when you left me, I was so weak-hearted as to take a long cry, because I could not get with you. But excuse a woman's weakness."

The reason for her "long cry" may, indeed, have been Emile's departure; but it is more likely to have been her increasing sense of helplessness and despair. She had been unable to tell Emile about Minnoch, either in person or in writing, and she had every reason to believe that Emile would not give up easily.

A letter postmarked January 23, 1857, betrayed a difference in Madeleine's perceptions of their late-night meetings: Emile's caresses were secondary now to her pressing need to talk with him. Before she could post the letter, however, Emile paid a surprise visit to her window.

> My Dear Emile,
>
> I was so very sorry that I could not see you tonight. I had expected an hour's chat with you—but we must just hope for better the next time.
>
> I hope you enjoyed the Ball.
>
> We had such a charming party at the Taylors. But the most horrid, low, vulgar set of people we had at the Tweedies'—people I never heard of. I was quite sick of them. If they send us fifty invitations, I shall never go to one of their parties again—neither shall Bessie.
>
> We had a most pressing invitation to go to the Ball tonight, but we declined.
>
> I don't see the least chance for [our wedding], my dear love. Mama is not well enough to go from home—and I don't see how we could manage in Edinburgh, because I could not leave a friend's house without their knowing it. So, sweet pet, it must at present be put off till a better time. Papa wishes us to put off our visit to Edinburgh till after the opera has been here. He has reserved our seats, I think.
>
> I am, with much love,
> forever your own fond Mimi L'Angelier.

P.S. [Sunday night]

Emile, my beloved, you have just left me. Oh, sweet darling, at this moment my heart and soul burn with love for thee, my husband, my own sweet one.

Emile, what would I not give at this moment to be your fond wife.

My nightdress was on when you saw me. Would to God you had been in the same attire. We would be happy. I do vex and annoy you, but, oh, sweet love, I do fondly love you with my soul.

I never felt so restless and so unhappy as I have done for some time past. I would do anything to keep sad thoughts from my mind. But in whatever place, some things make me feel sad. A dark spot is in the future. What can it be? Oh, God, keep it from us! Oh, may we be happy—dear darling, pray for our happiness. But alas, I see no chance of happiness for me. I *must* speak with you. Yes, I must again be pressed to your loving bosom—be kissed by you, my only love. Why were we fated to be so unhappy? Why were we made to be kept separate?

My heart is too full to write more. Oh, pardon, forgive me.

The "dark spot in the future" occurred on January 28, 1857: Minnoch formally proposed marriage and Madeleine accepted. She now found herself engaged to one man and "married" to another.

Soon after Minnoch's proposal, Madeleine wrote to Emile. Although she did not mention her recent engagement to Minnoch, Emile was in some way angered by the letter's content, and he returned the letter to her.

Initially, Madeleine was outraged at this insult, but she quickly saw his action as a possible escape from the entire problem of Emile. Her previous attempts to gradually ease out of their "marriage" had failed. Detailing her unworthiness and reminding him of his past loves had not achieved the desired result. Feeling time rapidly closing in around her, she changed tactics, and on Monday, February 2, wrote a dramatic and harsh letter to end their relationship.

I felt truly astonished to have my last letter returned to me. But it will be the last you shall have an opportunity of returning to me. When you are not pleased with the letters I send you, then our correspondence shall be at an end—and as there is coolness on both sides, our engagement had better be broken. This may astonish you, but you have more than once returned me my letters, and my mind was made up that I should not stand the same thing again. And you also annoyed me much on Saturday by your conduct in coming so near me.

Altogether, I think owing to coolness and indifference—nothing else—that we had better, for the future, consider ourselves as strangers.

I trust your honor as a gentleman that you will not reveal anything that may have passed between us. I shall feel obliged by your bringing me my letters and likeness on Thursday evening at seven. Be at the area gate, and Christina will take the parcel from you. On Friday night, I shall send you all your letters, likeness, etc.

I trust you may yet be happy, and get one more worthy of you than I. On Thursday, at seven o'clock.

I am, etc., M.

P.S. You may be astonished at this sudden change—but for some time back you must have noticed a coolness in my notes. My love for you has ceased, and that is why I was cool. I did once love you truly, fondly, but for some time back I have lost much of that love. There is no other reason for my conduct, and I think it but fair to let you know this. I might have gone on and become your wife, but I could not have loved you as I ought.

My conduct you will condemn, but I did at one time love you with heart and soul. It has cost me much to tell you this—sleepless nights—but it is necessary you should know. If you remain in Glasgow, or go away, I hope you may succeed in all you endeavors.

I know you will never injure the character of one you so fondly loved. No, Emile, I know you have honor and are a gentleman. What has passed you will not mention. I know when I ask you, that you will comply.

Adieu.

Her letter is full of fraud. Her engagement to Minnoch, and not a mutual "coolness and indifference—nothing else," was the reason for her wanting to end the relationship and recover her letters. Her correspondence during the preceding weeks, as previously noted, was perhaps more strained by the ever-growing presence of Minnoch, but was not dramatically less florid than her earlier letters—a postscript from a late January note began: "Oh, sweet darling, at this moment my heart and soul burn with love for thee, my husband, my own sweet one. Emile, what would I not give at this moment to be your fond wife."

Emile's friends and coworkers would later testify that he was despondent at the receipt of her abrupt letter. They encouraged Emile to return her letters and be done with her. But Emile, who had once enjoyed the drama of being the cast-off lover, would not repeat the role. For his own private reasons, he was not going to let this woman go. While deliberating his reply, he once again reacted in the way he knew would most torment her: complete silence.

A full week after her previous letter, early on February 9, she wrote to him again.

I attribute it to your having a cold that I had no answer to my last note. On Thursday evening you were, I suppose, afraid of the night air. I fear your cold is not better. I again appoint Thursday night—same place, street gate, seven o'clock.

- M.

P.S. If you cannot send me or bring me the parcel on Thursday, please write a note saying when you shall bring it—and address it to Christina. Send it by post.

Later that day, she received his response, the content of which can be easily discerned from her immediate reply.

Emile, I have just had your note.

Emile, for the love you once had for me, do nothing till I see you. For God's sake, do not bring your once-loved Mimi to an open shame.

Emile, I have deceived you. I have deceived my mother. God knows she did not boast of anything I had said of you—for she, poor woman, thought I had broken off with you last winter. I deceived you by telling you she still knew of our engagement. She did not. This I now confess—and as for wishing for any engagement with another, I do not fancy she ever thought of it.

Emile, write to no one—not to Papa or any other.

Oh, do not till I see you on Wednesday night. Be at the Hamiltons at twelve o'clock, and I shall open my shutter, and then you come to the area gate—I shall see you.

It would break my mother's heart.

Oh, Emile, be not harsh to me. I am the most guilty, miserable wretch on the face of the earth. Emile, do not drive me to death.

When I ceased to love you, believe me, it was not to love another. I am free from all engagement at present.

Emile, for God's sake do not send my letters to Papa. It will be an open rupture. I will leave the house. I will die. Emile, do nothing till I see you.

One word tomorrow night at my window to tell me—or I shall go mad.

Emile, you did love me. I did fondly, truly, love you too. Oh, dear Emile, be not so harsh to me. Will you not—but I cannot ask forgiveness. I am too guilty for that. I have deceived—it was love for you at the time [that] made me say Mama knew of our engagement.

Tomorrow one word—and on Wednesday we meet.

I would not again ask you to love me, for I know you could not. But, oh Emile, do not make me go mad.

I will tell you that only myself and Christina knew of my engagement to you. Mama did not know since last winter.

Pray for me—for a guilty wretch. But do nothing. Oh, Emile, do nothing.

Ten o'clock tomorrow night—one line, for the love of God.

P.S. [Tuesday morning]

I am ill. God knows what I have suffered. My punishment is more than I can bear.

Do nothing till I see you. For the love of heaven, do nothing.

I am mad. I am ill.

In the midst of her hysteria, she still possessed a clear enough state of mind to lie ("I am free from all engagement at present"), and she knew that she must do whatever was necessary to retrieve her personal, and, by that society's standards, very damning letters.

Emile answered her letter on the afternoon of February 10, and she replied directly.

Emile, I have this night received your note. Oh, it is kind of you to write to me.

Emile, no one can know the intense agony of mind I have suffered last night and today.

Emile, my father's wrath would kill me—you little know his temper. Emile, for the love you once had for me, do not denounce me to Papa. Emile, if he should read my letters to you—he will put me from him. He will hate me as a guilty wretch.

I loved you, and wrote to you in my first ardent love—it was with my deepest love I loved you. It was for your love I adored you.

I put on paper what I should not. I was free, because I loved you with my heart. If Papa or any other saw those fond letters to you, what would not be said of me? On my bended knees I write you, and ask you: as you hope for mercy at Judgment Day, do not inform on me. Do not make me a public shame.

Emile, my life has been one of bitter disappointment. You—and you only—can make the rest of my life peaceful. My own conscience will be a punishment that I shall carry to my grave. I have deceived the best of men. You may forgive me, but God never will. For God's love, forgive me. And betray me not—for the love you once had to me, do not bring down my father's wrath on me. It will kill my mother—who is not well. It will forever cause me bitter unhappiness. I am humble before you and crave your mercy. You can give me forgiveness—and you only can make me happy for the rest of my life.

I would not ask you to love me or ever make me your wife. I am too guilty for that. I have deceived and told you too many falsehoods for you ever to respect me. But will you not keep my secret from the world? Will you, for Christ's sake, not denounce me? I shall be undone. I shall be ruined. Who would trust me? Shame would be my lot. Despise me, hate me, but make me not the public scandal. Forget me ever, blot out all remembrance of me.

I did love you, and it was my soul's ambition to be your wife.

I asked you to tell me my faults. You did so, and it made me cool towards you gradually. When you have found fault with me, I have cooled. It was not love for another—for there is no one I love. My love has all been given to you. My heart is empty, cold—I am unloved. I am despised.

I told you I had ceased to love you—it was true. I did not love you as I did—but oh, till within the time of our coming back to Glasgow, I loved you fondly. I longed to be your wife. I had fixed [the wedding for] February. I longed for it. The time came, and I could not leave my father's house, and I grew discontented. Then I ceased to love you—oh, Emile, this is indeed the true statement. Now you can know my state of mind. Emile, I have suffered much for you. I lost much of my father's confidence since that September. And my mother has never been the same to me. No—she has never given me the same kind look. For the sake of my mother—she who gave me life—spare me from shame.

Oh, Emile, will you in God's name hear my prayer? I ask God to forgive me. I have prayed that He might put it in your heart yet to spare me from shame. Never, never while I live can I be happy. No—I shall always have the thought I deceived you. I am guilty. It will be a punishment I shall bear till the day of my death. I am humbled thus to crave your pardon. But I care not. While I have breath, I shall ever think of you as my best friend—if you will only keep this between ourselves. I blush to ask you. Yet, Emile, will you not grant me this, my last favor? If you will never reveal what has passed. Oh, for God's sake, for the love of heaven, hear me.

I grow mad. I have been ill, very ill, all day. I have had what has given me a false spirit. I had to resort to what I should not have taken, but my brain is on fire. I feel as if death would indeed be sweet.

Denounce me not. Emile, think of our once-happy days. Pardon me if you can, pray for me as the most wretched, guilty, miserable creature on Earth.

I could stand anything but my father's hot displeasure. Emile, you will not cause me death. If Papa is to get your letters, I cannot see him anymore. And my poor mother! I will never more kiss her—it would be a shame to them all.

Emile, will you not spare me this? Hate me—despise me—but do not expose me.

I cannot write more. I am too ill tonight.

M.

P.S. I cannot get to the back stair. I never could see the latch to it. I will take you within in the door. The area gate will be open. I shall see you from my window at twelve o'clock. I will wait till one o'clock.

Directly following the mailing of this letter, Madeleine sent the Smith family houseboy, William Murray, on a curious errand: to a local apothecary with a note requesting a small vial of prussic acid, with which, she said, she wanted to clean her hands. Prussic acid is a highly caustic substance and ingesting a few drops can readily kill a healthy adult. The apothecary refused to give the boy the poison, and Murray returned to the Smith home and related his experience to Madeleine. She told him to never mind, and went about her business. (In a jolting echo, Lizzie Borden would attempt to make a similar purchase of prussic acid thirty-five years later, on the day before her father and stepmother were murdered. Miss Borden needed it to "clean a sealskin coat." Her request, like Madeleine's, was denied.)

Madeleine's biographers have all hypothesized about the real intent behind her attempted prussic acid purchase. Some suggest that she intended to poison Emile with it, while others have speculated that she planned to use the substance to take her own life, should Emile actually reveal her letters to anyone. Nobody has given any credence to her stated purpose of "cleaning her hands."

A meeting had been arranged in the postscript of her last letter, and Madeleine and Emile did meet, perhaps more than once. No record exists of what was said between them, but her next known letter, sent on Valentine's Day, clearly shows that some form of reconciliation had been achieved—although her letters would never again contain the same level of affection, nor would she ever again refer to herself as Emile's "wife" or by the surname "L'Angelier."

Her endeavor to get back her letters had failed. By all outward appearances, she was now the happy fiancée of William Minnoch, but she was still secretly bound to Emile. The situation could not continue.

My Dear Emile,

I have got my finger cut, and cannot write—so, dear, I wish you would excuse me.

I was glad to see you looking so well yesterday. I hope to see you very soon.

Write me for next Thursday, and then I shall tell you when I can see you.

I want, the first time we meet, that you will bring me all my cool letters back—the last four I have written—and I will give you others in their place. Bring them all to me.

Excuse me more—just now it hurts me to write—so with kindness and dearest love, ever believe me, yours with love and affection,

M.

One morning in mid-February, Emile suffered the first occurrence of an illness marked by stomach cramps, nausea, and vomiting. He recovered quickly, and was well enough by the afternoon to go out.

Emile told Madeleine of his illness in a letter, and she responded in the next available post: "You did look bad Sunday night and Monday morning. I think you got sick with walking home so late—and the long want of food. So, the next time we meet I shall make you eat a loaf of bread before you go. . . . " This letter is undated, however, and it would be argued later that this passage could have been written at *any* time during their relationship, and did not specifically pertain to his first illness.

On February 21, Madeleine went to Murdoch's, a local apothecary, and bought sixpennyworth of arsenic. She told the clerk that the poison was needed to kill rats, and she signed the Poison Book, as was required by law. The book's notation read:

> *Miss Smith, 7 Blythswood Square, 6d. worth arsenic for garden and country house.*

She later asked why the arsenic was not pure white and was told that the law required it to be mixed with a coloring agent, usually indigo or soot—a precaution, most likely, to prevent the poison from being mistaken for sugar or flour or any other common food item.

It is not known if Emile and Madeleine met on the night of February 21, but on the morning of the 22nd, Emile experienced a second bout of the stomach illness, this one severe enough to keep him at home and convalescing for a week.

Madeleine wrote to Emile in early March, a chatty letter that only marginally concerned itself with his health.

MY DEAREST EMILE,

I hope by this time you are quite well and able to be out. I saw you at your window, but I could not tell how you looked—well, I hope.

I was in Edinburgh on Saturday to be at a luncheon party at the castle. It was a most charming day, and we enjoyed our trip very much.

On Friday we go to Stirling for a fortnight. I am so sorry, my dearest pet, I cannot see you ere we go—but I cannot.

Will you write me for Thursday, at eight o'clock, and I shall get it before I go—which will be a comfort to me—as I shall not hear from you till I come home again.

I will write you—but, sweet pet, it may only be once a week—as I have so many friends in that quarter.

Bessie is not going till next week. Mama, Papa, James, and I go on Friday. Bessie goes to the Ball next week. I am going to a Ball in Edinburgh the end of this week, so cannot go to both—and I would rather go to the one in Edinburgh.

I have not seen you all this week—have you been passing?

I have no news to give you. I am very well, and I think the next time we meet you will think I look better than I did the last time.

You won't have a letter from me this Saturday, as I shall be off—but I shall write the beginning of the week. Write me for Thursday, sweet love.

With love and affection,
MIMI.

Emile consulted his doctor about his recurring sickness, and the physician recommended that he go away to recuperate—perhaps to Bridge of Allan, a popular resort spa near Stirling where, coincidentally, the Smith family would be vacationing from March 6–17. Upon hearing of the doctor's advice, Madeleine urged Emile: "I hope you won't go to Bridge of Allan, as Papa and Mama would say it was I brought you there—and it would make me to feel very unhappy. Stirling you need not go to—as it is a nasty, dirty little town. Go [instead] to the Isle of Wight."

Madeleine failed to mention in her letter that William Minnoch would be a guest of the Smith family while they were on holiday.

A draft of Emile's response to the previous letter survives and, once again, it can be presumed that the final letter was very near it in tone and content. At question are rumors of Madeleine's engagement to Minnoch and the origin of a necklace Madeleine had worn during a late-night rendezvous with Emile. Gossip about both topics was being eagerly circulated by Mrs. Janet Anderson, a friend of the Smith family. Emile firmly stated his case and demanded answers.

MY DEAR, SWEET PET MIMI,

I feel indeed very vexed that the answer I received yesterday in response to my letter of Tuesday should prevent me from sending you the kind letter I had ready for you. You must not blame me for this, but your cold, indifferent and reserved notes—so short, without a particle of love in them—especially after pledging your word you were to write me kindly for those letters you asked me to destroy—and the manner you evaded answering the questions I put to you in my last letter—in combination with the reports I hear, fully convince me, Mimi, that there is foundation in your marriage with another. Besides, the way you put off our union till September without a just reason is very suspicious.

I do not think, Mimi dear, that Mrs. Anderson would say your mother told her things she had not—and I could never believe Mr. Houldsworth would be guilty of telling a falsehood for mere talking. No, Mimi, there is a foundation for all this.

You often go to Mr. Minnoch's house, and common sense would lead anyone to believe that if you were not on the footing reports say you are—you would avoid going near any of his friends. I know he goes with you, or at least will meet you, in Stirlingshire.

Mimi, dear, place yourself in my position and tell me: am I wrong in believing what I hear?

I was happy the last time we met—yes, very happy. I was forgetting all the past, but now it is again beginning.

Mimi, I insist on having an explicit answer to the questions you evaded in my last letter. If you evade answering them this time, I must try some other means of coming to the truth. If not answered in a satisfactory manner, you must not expect I shall again write you personally or meet you when you return home. I do not wish you to answer this at random. I shall wait a day or so if you require it. I know you cannot write me from Stirlingshire, as the time you have to write me a letter is occupied in doing so to others. There was a time you would have found plenty of time.

Answer me this, Mimi: who gave you the trinket you showed me? Is it true it was Mr. Minnoch? And is it true that you are, directly or indirectly, engaged to Mr. Minnoch or to anyone else but me? These questions I must know.

The doctor says I must go to Bridge of Allan. I cannot travel five-hundred miles to the Isle of Wight and five-hundred back. What is your objective in wishing me so very much to go south? I may not go to Bridge of Allan till Wednesday. If I can avoid going, I shall do so for your sake. I shall wait to hear from you.

I hope, dear, nothing will happen to check the happiness we were again enjoying.

May God bless you, pet, and with many fond and tender embraces, believe me with kind love your ever affectionate husband,

EMILE L'ANGELIER.

Madeleine responded with a brief letter written a few days before the Smith family left for Bridge of Allan:

MY SWEET, DEAR PET,

I am so sorry you should be so vexed. Believe nothing, sweet one, till I tell you myself.

It is a report I am sorry about, but it has been six months spoken of. There is one of the same kind about Bessie. Believe nothing till I tell you—I love you and you only.

Mrs. Anderson only supposed—Mama never told her—but we have found out that Mrs. Anderson is very good at making up stories. Mrs. Anderson asked me if it was Minnoch gave me the trinket you saw—and I told her no. My sweet love, I love you, and only wish you were better. We shall speak of our union when we meet.

We shall be home about the 17th, so I may see you about that time. I wish, love, you could manage to remain in town till we come home, as I know it will be a grand row with Papa and me if you are seen at Bridge of Allan. Could you, sweet love, not wait for my sake till we come home? You might go the 20th or so. I would be so pleased with you if you can do this to please me, my own dear beloved.

I have quarreled with Christina just now—so cannot see you tonight. I shall write you next week.

Neither Minnoch nor his sisters go with us—only Mama, Bessie, James, and I go tomorrow—Papa on Saturday night.

I have only been in Minnoch's house once, and that was this week: I was taking a message, because Mama could not go herself.

I will tell and answer you all questions when we meet.

On the morning of March 6, the day of the Smiths' departure, Madeleine and Mary Jane Buchanan, a friend of Madeleine's since their London school days together, strolled among the busy shopping of Sauchiehall Street. The young ladies discussed, among other topics, Mary Jane's intended role as bridesmaid at Madeleine and Minnoch's wedding. As they came to Currie's apothecary, Madeleine asked her friend to step into the shop with her, where Madeleine made a second purchase of sixpennyworth of arsenic, again stating that she needed it to kill rats. The clerk cautioned her as to the danger of the substance, to which Madeleine replied that it would be perfectly safe, since everybody would be away from home when she set it out. She signed the Poison Book, and Madeleine and Mary Jane walked back out into the bustling crowds.

As Madeleine had requested, Emile decided to avoid Bridge of Allan during the time when the Smith family would be there. He did not, however, tell Madeleine of his new travel itinerary, leaving her unaware of his exact location and schedule. This omission of information would play a considerable part in the events of the following two weeks.

On March 12, while at Bridge of Allan, Madeleine and William Minnoch set their wedding date for June 18, 1857. In a March 13 letter sent to Emile in Glasgow, there was no trace of the panic Madeleine must have been feeling. A wedding was now formally in the works, and Madeleine knew word would spread quickly—as neither her family nor Minnoch knew of any reason to hide the happy news.

DEAREST & BELOVED,

I hope you are well. I am very well, and anxious to get home to see you, sweet one.

It is cold, and we have had snow all the week, which is most disagreeable.

I feel better since we came here.

I think we shall be home on Tuesday, so I shall let you know, when we shall have a dear, sweet interview, when I may be pressed to your heart and kissed by you.

I hope you will enjoy your visit here. You will find it so dull, no one here we know, and I don't fancy you will find any friends, as they are all strangers, and don't appear nice people. I wish we had not come here for another month—as it would have been so much nicer—it would then be warm. I think if you could wait a little to come here, it would do you more good—but only you know best when you can get away.

Adieu. Ever yours, with love and fond kisses,
MIMI.

This letter had to be forwarded, because, unknown to Madeleine, Emile had gone to Edinburgh on March 10 to begin his convalescence and to visit Mary Perry's sister and brother-in-law.

Having formally accepted his proposal of marriage, Madeleine sent William Minnoch an affectionate note after he had returned to Glasgow. The restrained tone in her letter is very much the proper one for a young Victorian lady writing to her intended groom—and consequently it is unlike any letter she had written to Emile.

MY DEAREST WILLIAM,

It is but fair, after your kindness to me, that I should write you a note.

The day I part from friends I always feel sad. But to part from one I love, as I do you, makes me feel truly sad and dull. My only consolation is that we shall meet soon.

Tomorrow we shall be home. I do so wish you were here today. We might take a long walk. Our walk to Dunblane I shall ever remember with pleasure. That walk fixed a day on which we are to begin a new life—a life which I hope may be of happiness and long duration to both of us. My aim through life shall be to please you and study you.

Dear William, I must conclude, as Mama is ready to go to Stirling. I do not go with the same pleasure as I did the last time. I hope you got to town safe, and found your sisters well.

Accept my warmest, kindest love and ever believe me to be
yours with affection,
MADELEINE.

Madeleine's aim to "please you and study you" sounds a striking echo of her letter from the previous summer, where she vowed to Emile: "it will be my constant endeavor to please you and to add to your comfort. I shall try to study you, and when you get a little out of temper, I shall try and pet you, dearest—kiss and fondle you."

The Smith family returned home, as planned, on the afternoon of March 17. Emile returned from Edinburgh the same day, and was disappointed to find no letter from Madeleine waiting for him.

The following day, Madeleine returned to Currie's and purchased a third sixpennyworth of arsenic, saying the previous quantity had proven very effective in killing the rats.

Having no letter from Madeleine to respond to, Emile left for Bridge of Allan early on Thursday, the nineteenth, without informing her of his departure. He asked one of the other boarders at Mrs. Jenkins's, a Frenchman named

Amadee Thuau, to forward any incoming letters to the Post Office at Bridge of Allan. Soon after his departure, a letter from Madeleine arrived, and Thuau forwarded it on, so Emile would receive it that afternoon.

On Friday, March 20, he wrote letters to his supervisor, William Stevenson ("Are you very busy? Am I wanted?"), to his coworker, Tom Kennedy ("[this] place is worth seeing—but as dull as a chimney can."), and to Mary Perry.

> Dear Mary,
>
> I should have written to you before, but I am so lazy writing when away from my ordinary ways.
>
> I feel much better, and I hope to be home the middle of next week.
>
> This is a very stupid place—very dull. I know no one—and besides, it is so very much colder than Edinburgh.
>
> I saw your friends in Portbello, and will tell you about them when I see you.
>
> I should have come [back to Glasgow] to see someone last night, but the letter came too late, so we are both disappointed.
>
> Trusting you are quite well, and with kind regards to yourself and your sister,
>
> > believe me, yours sincerely,
> > P. Emile L'Angelier.
>
> P.S. I shall be here till Wednesday.

All of Madeleine's biographers agree that "I should have come [back to Glasgow] to see someone last night . . ." refers to Madeleine, although it is peculiar that he does not refer to her by name to Mary Perry, a confidante for almost all of the details of their courtship. The letter that "came too late" was never recovered (although the envelope was), but it apparently outlined Madeleine's proposed plans for a meeting. Curiously, he did not reply to her letter.

Madeleine, still believing that Emile was in Glasgow, was puzzled by his silence and by his absence at the meeting she had arranged in her letter. She wrote another letter and mailed it to him at Mrs. Jenkins's. It would be the final letter to pass between them.

> Why, my beloved, did you not come to me? Oh, beloved, are you ill? Come to me, sweet one.
>
> I waited and waited for you, but you came not. I shall wait again tomorrow night—same hour and arrangement.

Do come, sweet love, my own dear love of a sweetheart. Come, beloved, and clasp me to your heart. Come, and we shall be happy.

A kiss, fond love.

Adieu, with tender embraces, ever believe me to be your own ever dear,
fond MIMI.

When this letter arrived on Saturday, March 21, Mrs. Jenkins passed it along to Amadee Thuau, who forwarded it to Emile with a brief note saying that the letter had arrived before noon on Saturday. Emile received the forwarded letter at the Bridge of Allan Post Office on the morning of Sunday, March 22. As the letter was undated, and the postmark of Madeleine's envelope read *Glasgow, 21 Mr 1857*, Emile apparently concluded that the "tomorrow night" referenced in the letter indicated Sunday night. He quickly made arrangements to catch the first train back to Glasgow.

He arrived back at his lodgings at about eight o'clock on Sunday evening. Mrs. Jenkins was surprised to see him, as she had not expected him to return until the middle of the coming week. He told her that a letter had brought him back early. After a quick meal of tea and toast, he asked Mrs. Jenkins for the pass key to the front door, saying he intended to be out late. He also asked her to wake him early the following morning, as he would return to Bridge of Allan by an early train.

James Galloway, a casual acquaintance, saw Emile walking east on Sauchiehall Street, which is north of Blythswood Square, at approximately nine o'clock that night. It was too early for the usual meeting time with Madeleine. The Smith household was awake and engaged in their customary Sunday night prayers.

At 9:20 that evening, Emile arrived at Mrs. Parr's lodging house on St. Vincent Street, to the south of Blythswood Square. He asked after his friend, Mr. McAlester, but the maid informed him that McAlester was not at home, and she watched Emile walk back out into the darkened Glasgow streets.

Emile then vanished for a full five hours, his whereabouts and history unknown until Mrs. Jenkins was awoken by the clamor of doorbells in the early hours of Monday, March 23.

Madeleine Smith
(based on the 1857 newspaper original)

Emile L'Angelier
(based on the 1857 newspaper original)

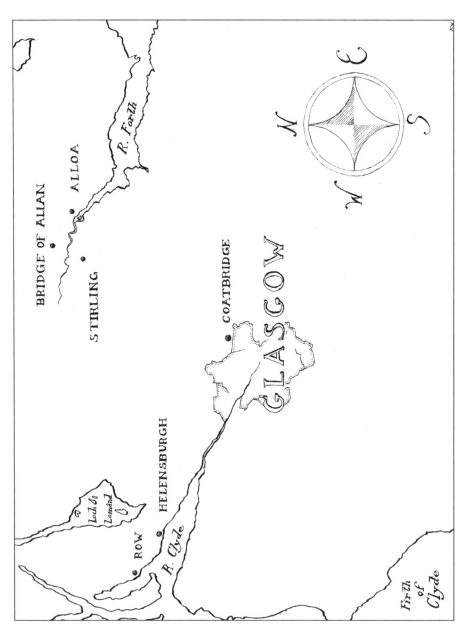

Glasgow and environs, 1857

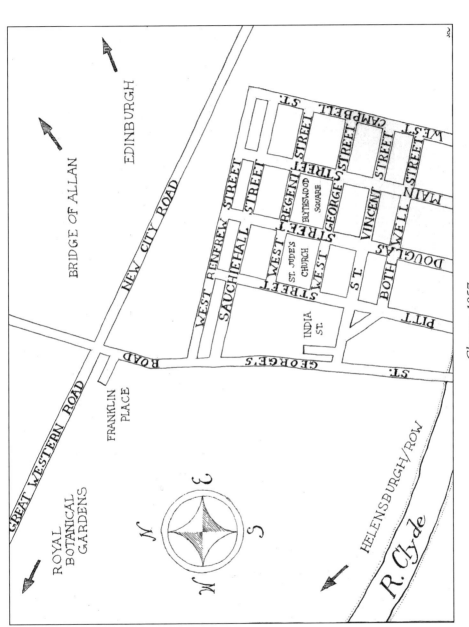

Glasgow, 1857

February 1857

Sun	Mon	Tue	Wed	Thu	Fri	Sat
1	2 Madeleine writes harsh letter to Emile, ending their relationship	3	4	5	6	7
8	9 Emile threatens to show Madeleine's letters to her father	10 Madeleine sends letter to Emile, begging for mercy	11	12 Emile's first illness?	13	14
			Madeleine tries to purchase prussic acid			
15	16	17	18	19 Emile's first illness?	20	21 Madeleine's first arsenic purchase
22	23	24	25	26	27	28
			Emile's second illness			

March 1857

Sun	Mon	Tue	Wed	Thu	Fri	Sat
1	2	3	4	5	6 Madeleine's second arsenic purchase	7
8	9	10	11	12	13	14
				Emile in Edinburgh		
		The Smith family at Bridge of Allan				
15	16	17	18 Madeleine's third arsenic purchase	19	20	21
				Emile at Bridge of Allan		
22	23 Emile dies	24 first postmortem of Emile's body	25	26 Madeleine flees to Row Emile buried	27	28
29	30	31 second postmortem of Emile's body Madeleine arrested				

Part VI

The Trial of the Century

MISS MARY PERRY arrived at Emile's lodging house not long after he had been pronounced dead. The reason he had summoned her, whatever he had wanted to make known, would never come to light. Mrs. Jenkins initially believed Miss Perry to be the fiancée Emile had spoken of, but Miss Perry corrected her, saying she was just a friend. Mrs. Jenkins showed the visitor to Emile's room, where Miss Perry was overcome with grief and kissed Emile's still warm forehead.

After leaving Emile's lodgings, Mary Perry went directly to the Smith home and told the maid who answered the door that she needed to see Madeleine's mother. As the servant went to fetch Mrs. Smith, Madeleine came into the hall and, surprised to see Perry in her house, smiled and asked if anything was wrong. Perry said she needed to speak with her mother, so Madeleine showed her into the sitting room and left through the doorway just as Mrs. Smith entered. What the two older women discussed has never been disclosed, and Miss Perry was never asked about the details of their confidential conversation during the course of the investigation or at the trial.

Emile's death was duly reported to his employers at Huggins by a druggist named Chrystal, who had been called for by Mrs. Jenkins. On hearing the news, William Stevenson, Emile's direct supervisor at Huggins, went to the office of French Consul de Mean, whom he knew to be a friend of Emile's. At de Mean's office, Stevenson encountered Amadee Thuau, Emile's fellow lodger, who gave Stevenson the few details he knew in a distraught mixture of French and English.

Accompanying Thuau back to Mrs. Jenkins's, Stevenson was asked by the landlady to take responsibility for the belongings in Emile's room. Going through Emile's desk, he found several stacks of letters, assorted keys, and a small notebook. Putting these aside, Stevenson then went through the clothes Emile had been wearing on his return from Bridge of Allan. In one of the pockets he found a folded piece of paper: Madeleine's final letter. Reading it, he exclaimed to those in the room (Mrs. Jenkins, Thuau, and Emile's regular physician, Dr. Thomson) that he now understood why Emile had come back unexpectedly from Bridge of Allan.

Stevenson left the keys and letters on top of the desk, but took the notebook with him back to his office. In an attempt to find Emile's mother's address in Jersey, Stevenson and Thomas Kennedy unlocked Emile's desk at Huggins and searched its contents. The drawers were full of loose piles of letters and two packages of correspondence wrapped in brown paper and sealed with the company's stamp—security measures taken by Emile himself. After sifting through the papers, Stevenson placed all the letters and the notebook into the drawers, locked the desk, and left the key with Kennedy.

Monsieur de Mean went to visit Mr. James Smith on the evening of March 23. Emile had previously told de Mean of his extensive correspondence with Madeleine, and may even have spoken of the couple's sexual intimacy. De Mean warned the elder Smith to take every precaution so that the letters did not fall into a stranger's hands.

De Mean went a step further the following morning and went to Emile's office to request possession of the letters from his desk. William Stevenson refused, saying to release them he would need the permission of Mr. Huggins, who was unavailable. Frustrated, de Mean told Stevenson to keep the letters sealed and locked—and unread—until they could be properly disposed of.

Stevenson, in all probability, reported this encounter to Mr. Huggins. Huggins, either suspicious of the French Consul's interest in the correspondence of a common clerk, or else feeling an obligation to Emile as a valued employee, authorized payment for a postmortem exam of Emile's body. Stevenson asked Dr. Steven to perform the procedure, and, with the assistance of Dr. Thomson, Steven examined Emile's body at noon on Tuesday the 24th, the day after Emile's death.

In the course of their examination, Emile's abdomen was opened and his stomach removed. The appearance of various inner organs made both doctors suspect the presence of some form of poison, and the stomach and its contents were put into jars for additional analysis at a later time. The results of their examination were given to Stevenson to pass along to Huggins and to anyone else Huggins wished to inform.

On Wednesday, March 25, William Stevenson brought the written results of the postmortem to the office of the Procurator-Fiscal, the legal public prosecutor. The Fiscal read the document and then asked for a sample of the correspondence that was in Emile's possession at the time of his death. Stevenson retrieved several of Madeleine's letters and left them in the Fiscal's custody.

Emile's death notice appeared in Wednesday's *North British Daily Mail*, at the request of Mr. Huggins.

Monsieur de Mean returned to see James Smith on Wednesday and reported his failure to obtain Madeleine's letters from Emile's employer. At Mr. Smith's request, de Mean then went to speak with Madeleine. In the presence of her mother, de Mean questioned Madeleine about her knowledge of Emile's final hours and death. Madeleine swore emphatically that she had not seen Emile for several weeks, and, in fact, until de Mean himself mentioned it to her, she did not even know that Emile had been away from Glasgow in the previous weeks.

She further explained that when she wrote Emile that final letter on the evening of Friday, March 20, she proposed a rendezvous for the following night, Saturday the 21st—and not Sunday the 22nd. Had he been in Glasgow, as she presumed he was, he would have received the letter on Saturday morning and known that "tomorrow night" referenced Saturday night. But if he did not receive the letter until Sunday and then interpreted "tomorrow night" to mean Sunday night, that was a misunderstanding on Emile's part, caused by the additional time it took for her letter to be forwarded to him.

When questioned further, Madeleine said that Emile had never set foot inside the Blythswood Square house, but admitted that she had sometimes spoken to him through her open bedroom window. Her purpose in writing the final letter, she told de Mean, was to set a time to meet with Emile so she could inform him of her engagement to William Minnoch and ask for the return of all her letters.

William Minnoch, oblivious to Madeleine's possible involvement in the death of a man he had probably never heard of, escorted Madeleine to a dinner on Wednesday night at the household of Mr. Middleton, the minister of the Smith family's church.

Thursday morning, March 26, young Janet Smith awoke to find her sister, Madeleine, gone from the bed they shared, gone from their room, and gone from the entire house.

In the chilly morning air, after a sparsely attended funeral held at Glasgow's Ramshorn Church, Emile's body was lowered into its final resting place—although he would rest there for less than a week.

William Minnoch stopped by the Smith home late Thursday morning to pay a call on his intended bride. Finding the family and servants in a panic, and hearing that Madeleine was missing, he suggested that she might have gone to Rowaleyn. The family agreed this was possible, and Minnoch proposed that he and Madeleine's brother Jack, travel to Row—the rest of the family remaining at home, in case she returned.

Minnoch and Jack took the next train from Glasgow to Greenock, and there caught a steamer headed for Helensburgh. Moving through the crowds of people on the boat, they found Madeleine sitting calmly and looking out at the water. She had boarded the boat earlier, in Glasgow, and showed no particular surprise at seeing the two of them. Sitting down next to her, Minnoch gently asked her why she had fled and caused such worry to her family and friends. She began to respond, but Minnoch told her to wait, as there were too many people about who might overhear.

The steamer docked at Helensburgh, and Madeleine, Jack, and Minnoch went on to Rowaleyn. In the privacy of the large house, Minnoch asked again for the reason behind her flight. Madeleine merely told him that she was afraid her parents would be very upset at what she had done, and promised to tell him more at a later time. During a long carriage ride broken by only infrequent conversation, the three rode back to the candlelit windows and gas lamps of a Glasgow evening.

On Friday the 27th, the jar containing Emile's stomach was sent for detailed analysis to Dr. Frederick Penny, a professor of Chemistry at the Andersonian University in Glasgow. That same morning, William Stevenson took a train to Bridge of Allan to collect the belongings that Emile had left at his vacation lodgings there: a leather case, hat, cigarette case, traveling bag, dressing case, and a travel blanket. After packing them into boxes, he asked the landlady to have everything shipped to Huggins.

On Saturday the 28th, William Minnoch called on Madeleine to see if she had recovered from Thursday's events and to ask again for the rationale behind her running away. Madeleine evaded the question, but eventually responded that she had written "a Frenchman" a letter, asking for the return of some correspondence she had written to him.

The morning of Monday, March 30, Emile's belongings arrived at Huggins from Bridge of Allan. William Stevenson found several additional letters within and, combining these with the letters locked in Emile's desk, he carefully noted on the envelopes (or on the letters themselves, if the envelopes were missing) where he had found each individual letter.

Soon after completing his inventory, Stevenson was interrupted by John Murray, a sheriff officer in Glasgow, and Bernard MacLauchlin, Murray's assistant. As legal representatives, they had come to take possession of all the papers in Emile's desk and those from the boxes recently arrived from Bridge of Allan. With Stevenson and Thomas Kennedy as official witnesses, Murray sealed the stacks of letters, and then asked Stevenson to accompany MacLauchlin and himself to Mrs. Jenkins's house, in order to gather Emile's collection of letters that remained there.

It was late in the day when the threesome collected the last of the papers from Emile's rented room. Rather than return to his office and then set out for home long past nightfall, Murray told MacLauchlin to take the letters they had found in Emile's lodgings home overnight and then bring them to the office the following morning.

Tuesday morning found William Minnoch once again paying a call at the Smith house—this time to see Mrs. Smith, whom he had heard was ill. He met Madeleine by chance in the hall, and she told him that her mother was too unwell to receive visitors. In the course of their brief conversation, Madeleine mentioned Emile by name, saying it was rumored that his death was caused by poisoning. She confided to Minnoch that she had, on occasion, purchased arsenic for cosmetic uses, something she had learned while at school in London.

At noon on that day, based upon the postmortem report and the contents of Madeleine's letters, Procurator-Fiscal James Hart issued a warrant for the arrest of Madeleine Hamilton Smith.

Also on Tuesday, William Wilson, an assistant in the Fiscal's office, took possession of all of Madeleine's letters, including those that had been at MacLauchlin's residence the previous night, and dutifully locked them up as evidence.

Archibald Smith, Sheriff-Substitute of Lanarkshire, took Madeleine into custody on Tuesday afternoon and recorded her statement concerning her possible involvement in Emile's death. The resulting document, her Declaration, would be Madeleine's sole voice in all upcoming legal proceedings, as Scottish law at the time forbade a defendant from actually taking the stand or issuing any statements during the trial. Instead, defendants had to rely entirely on their defense lawyers to speak for them.

Her Declaration, in its entirety, reads:

> My name is Madeleine Smith. I am a native of Glasgow; twenty-one years of age, and I reside with my father, James Smith, architect, at No. 7 Blythswood Square, Glasgow.
>
> For about the last two years I have been acquainted with P. Emile L'Angelier, who was in the employment of W. B. Huggins & Company, in Bothwell Street, and who lodged at 11 Franklin Place. He recently paid his addresses to me, and I have met with him on a variety of occasions.
>
> I learned about his death on the afternoon of Monday, the 23rd of March current, from Mama, to whom it had been mentioned by a lady, named Miss Perry, a friend of Mr. L'Angelier. I had not seen Mr. L'Angelier for about three weeks before his death, and the last time I saw him was on a

night about half-past ten o'clock. On that occasion he tapped at my bedroom window, which is on the ground floor and fronts Main Street. I talked to him from the window, which is stanchioned outside, and I did not go out to him nor did he come in to me. This occasion, which, as already said, was about three weeks before his death, was the last time I saw him.

He was in the habit of writing notes to me, and I was in the habit of replying to him by notes. The last note I wrote to him was on the Friday before his death—viz., Friday the 20th March current. I now see and identify that note and the relative envelope, and they are each marked *Number One*. In consequence of that note, I expected him to visit me on Saturday night the 21st current, at my bedroom window in the same way as formerly mentioned, but he did not come and sent no notice. There was no tapping at my window on said Saturday night or on the following night, being Sunday. I went to bed on Sunday night about eleven o'clock, and remained in bed till the usual time of getting up next morning, being eight or nine o'clock.

In the course of my meetings with Mr. L'Angelier, he and I had arranged to get married, and we had at one time proposed September last as the time the marriage was to take place, and subsequently the present month of March was spoken of. It was proposed that we should reside in furnished lodgings; but we had not made any definite arrangement as to time or otherwise.

He was very unwell for some time, and had gone to the Bridge of Allan for his health, and he complained of sickness, but I have no idea what was the cause of it.

I remember giving him some cocoa from my window one night some time ago, but I cannot specify the time particularly. He took the cup in his hand and barely tasted the contents, and I gave him no bread to it. I was taking some cocoa myself at the time, and had prepared it myself. It was between ten o'clock and eleven o'clock in the evening when I gave it to him.

I am now shown a note or letter and envelope which are marked respectively *Number Two*, and I recognize them as a note and envelope which I wrote to Mr. L'Angelier, and sent to the post. As I had attributed his sickness for want of food, I proposed, as stated in the note, to give him a loaf of bread—but I said that merely in a joke, and, in point of fact, I never gave him any bread.

I have bought arsenic on various occasions. The last I bought was a sixpenceworth, which I bought in Currie the apothecary's in Sauchiehall Street, and, prior to that, I bought other two quantities of arsenic, for which I paid sixpence each—one of these in Currie's, and the other in Murdoch the apothecary's shop, in Sauchiehall Street. I used it all as a cosmetic, and applied it to my face, neck, and arms, diluted with water. The arsenic I got in Currie's shop I got there on Wednesday the 18th March, and I used it all on one occasion, having put it all in the basin where I was to wash myself. I had been advised to the use of the arsenic in the way I have mentioned by a young lady, the daughter of an actress, and I had also seen the use of it recommended in the newspapers. The young lady's name was Guibilei, and I had met her at school at Clapton, near London.

I did not wish any of my father's family to be aware that I was using the arsenic, and therefore never mentioned it to any of them, and I don't suppose they or any of the servants ever noticed any of it in the basin. When I bought the arsenic in Murdoch's, I am not sure whether I was asked or not what it was for, but I think I said it was for a gardener to kill rats or destroy vermin about flowers, and I only said this because I did not wish them to know that I was going to use it as a cosmetic. I don't remember whether I was asked as to the use I was going to make of the arsenic on the other two occasions, but I likely made the same statement about it as I had done in Murdoch's—and on all the three occasions, as required in the shops, I signed my name to a book in which the sales were entered.

On the first occasion I was accompanied by Mary, a daughter of Dr. Buchanan of Dumbarton.

For several years past Mr. Minnoch, of the firm of William Houldsworth and Company, has been coming a good deal about my father's house, and about a month ago Mr. Minnoch made a proposal of marriage to me, and I gave him my hand in token of acceptance—but no time for the marriage has yet been fixed, and my object in writing the note *Number One*, before mentioned, was to have a meeting with Mr. L'Angelier to tell him that I was engaged in marriage to Mr. Minnoch.

I am now shown two notes and an envelope bearing the Glasgow postmark of 23 January, which are respectively marked *Number Three*, and I recognize these as in my handwriting, and they were written and sent by me to Mr. L'Angelier.

On the occasion that I gave Mr. L'Angelier the cocoa, as formerly mentioned, I think that I used it must have been known to the servants and members of my father's family, as the package containing the cocoa was lying on the mantelpiece in my room—but no one of the family used it except myself, as they did not seem to like it. The water which I used I got hot from the servants.

On the night of the 18th, when I used the arsenic last, I was going to a dinner party at Mr. Minnoch's house.

I never administered, or caused to be administered, to Mr. L'Angelier arsenic or anything injurious. And this I declare to be truth.

(*signed*) Madeleine Smith

By order of the Fiscal, on the same afternoon that Madeleine was giving her Declaration, Drs. Penny, Thomson, Steven, and Robert Telfer Corbet, another Glasgow physician, exhumed Emile's body. The four doctors performed a lengthy dissection and examination of the corpse in the forbidding stillness of Ramshorn Church. Their analysis would show arsenic in the intestines, rectum, liver, and brain of the dead man. Everything removed from the cadaver was placed into jars and given to Dr. Penny for further examination.

The local newspapers initially said nothing of the events surrounding Emile's death, until the April 3 edition of the *Glasgow Herald* began what would become a volcano of articles about the case:

"For the last few days the recital of an event of the most painful character has been passing from mouth to mouth, and has become the subject of almost universal excitement and inquiry. So long as the matter was confined to rumour and surmise, we did not consider that we were called on to make any public allusion to it; but now that a young lady has been committed to prison on a most serious charge, and the names of the respective parties are in the mouths of everyone, any further delicacy in the way of withholding allusion to the case is impossible. At the same time we fervently trust that the cloud which at present obscures a most respectable and estimable household may be speedily and most effectually removed."

James Smith, head of that "most respectable and estimable household," reacted to his daughter's arrest by obtaining the services of a team of lawyers headed by John Wilkie, a prominent Glasgow solicitor. Smith explained that Wilkie's job was two-fold: to give Madeleine the best legal representation possible, and to keep the rest of the Smith family far removed from the scandalous mess.

Seeking to limit the time the Crown's prosecution team would have to build a case against his client, the first action Wilkie took was a legal tactic called *running her letters*, which, as the *North British Mail* explained to its readers, meant "she must be indicted within 60 days, tried within 40 more, or discharged." Madeleine's trial would have to take place by July 9, 1857, at the very latest.

Preparations for the trial began immediately, with both the defense and prosecution working night and day to formulate a solid case. Tidbits of their stratagem and the unfolding evidence were leaked and duly reported to a gossip-hungry populace. The *Morning Advertiser* proclaimed: "All sorts of rumours are afloat bearing on the character of Miss Smith and the young Frenchman L'Angelier, whom she is accused of having poisoned. . . . It is said that the evidence at the trial will be of a very startling nature—so much indeed that it may be deemed advisable to conduct the case with closed doors."

In early April, Sheriff Murray gathered all the medicine bottles and other personal effects from Emile's room in Mrs. Jenkins's house. The Fiscal's office returned all of the collected letters to Murray and instructed him to label them as to where each one had been found. Based on Madeleine's Declaration, the prosecution and the defense wrote to doctors throughout Scotland, requesting their learned opinions on the various uses of arsenic—specifically inquiring if they had ever heard of the substance being used as a cosmetic. The Poison Books of apothecaries in Glasgow, Stirling, Bridge of Allan, and all points in-between were searched for purchases of arsenic by Emile or additional purchases by Madeleine. None were found.

Madeleine spent her time in Glasgow's North Prison by reading, keeping up with her correspondence, receiving visitors, and repeatedly asking the prison officials if she might have access to a piano.

The *Daily Express* reported a slightly different scene: " . . . When her father used to visit her shortly after her commitment to prison, he was looking as might naturally be expected, very gloomy and dull, but his lively daughter did not seem at all to share his feelings. 'Cheer up, Papa,' she said. 'Cheer up; it'll all be right soon.' Her medical attendant declares, however, this gaiety of nature is all assumed, for her pulse, he said, was beating at upwards of 100 in a minute."

In true Victorian fashion, Madeleine's family continued on as normal: Mr. Smith keeping all business appointments, and Mrs. Smith and Bessie keeping all social ones. Except for Mr. Smith's infrequent visits to the prison, the Smiths actively distanced themselves from Madeleine and the developing legal proceedings.

On June 13, Madeleine was officially served an indictment on three counts: two counts of attempted murder by arsenic, corresponding to Emile's first two bouts with the stomach illness, and one count of murder by arsenic. She barely glanced at the envelope, passing it unopened to one of the legal representatives in the room with her.

Legal authorities decided that her trial would be best moved from Glasgow, and Madeleine and her belongings were quietly transferred to Edinburgh's East Jail on June 24.

Daily newspapers had reported almost hourly on the progress of the case, presenting both real and highly imaginary facts. Editorial opinions and readers' impassioned letters were printed by the hundreds. Consequently, the first morning of the trial, June 30, 1857, saw the Edinburgh courtroom, the courthouse hallways, and the courtyard outside overflowing with reporters and the curious.

Madeleine's trial was presided over by the Lord Justice-Clerk, the Right Honorable John Hope. Assisting him in overseeing the case were Lord James Ivory and Lord Robert Handyside. The jury consisted of fifteen male jurors.

The lead prosecutor for the Crown, the Lord Advocate, was James Moncreiff, the forty-six-year-old son of the Ninth Baron of Tullibole. Highly regarded for his sharp legal mind, he would hold the title of Lord Advocate for a total of thirteen years during his judiciary career.

The primary counsel for the defense was the Dean of Faculty, John Inglis, the forty-seven-year-old son of a minister who had earned a reputation as a genius in Scotland's courtrooms. John Wilkie, who was not highly experienced in courtroom presentation, had stepped back after preparing Madeleine's case and only rarely participated in the actual trial.

As the audience waited restlessly for the trial to begin, the courtroom was crowded and noisy, with various legal clerks hurrying among the desks, distributing stacks of papers and official documents. The judges and lawyers then entered, took their seats, and the fervent conversations began to die down. The voices then vanished entirely: a trapdoor in the floor opened and Madeleine ascended, wearing a brown silk gown, lavender gloves, and a white bonnet with a veil. She carried a small vial of smelling salts, as was customary for women standing trial for such crimes, although Madeleine would never feel the need to use the vial during the course of the nine-day trial.

The court was called to session. The judges asked Archibald Smith, the Sheriff-Substitute of Lanarkshire, and George Gray, a clerk for the Sheriff's office, to verify their accurate obtaining of Madeleine's Declaration. The two pledged they had been meticulous in that work, Sheriff Smith adding: "Her answers were given clearly and distinctly. There was no appearance of hesitation or reserve. There was a great appearance of frankness and candor."

The indictment was then read aloud:

1. intent to murder on 19 or 20 February, 1857

2. intent to murder on 22 or 23 February, 1857

3. murder on 22 or 23 March, 1857

Madeleine stood and responded clearly: "Not guilty." This was the final time she would ever speak on the topic of Emile L'Angelier.

Lacking an eyewitness to link Madeleine with Emile on the night of his death, Moncreiff brought witnesses to the witness box, over the course of five and a quarter days, who would speak on seven different themes of circumstantial evidence:

- Emile's final weeks and hours

- Emile's character and history

- medical evidence

- the Smith household

- Madeleine's character and history

- Madeleine's arsenic purchases

- the handling of the documents presented as evidence

 The testimonies of the witnesses have been grouped according to theme and edited for brevity.

Moncreiff began the presentation of his case with Mrs. Ann Jenkins, who would speak on several of the seven themes and would relate, in great detail, the events as she remembered them.

"I am the wife of David Jenkins, and live at Number 11 Franklin Place, Glasgow. I knew the late Mr. L'Angelier. He lodged in my house. He first came to me about the end of July. He remained in my house as a lodger until his death. His usual habits were civil—but he was in the habit of staying out at night—although not very often."

On the topic of Emile's social life, Mrs. Jenkins told of his correspondences and economical entertainments: "He was in the habit of receiving a great many letters, but I thought they were addressed in a gentleman's hand. There were a great many letters in the same hand. Sometimes they came in yellow, and sometimes, I think, in white envelopes. He never told me whom these letters were from. I never thought the letters came from a lady. He never said anything to me about taking in these letters." When shown several of the envelopes collected by the Sheriff and Fiscal, Mrs. Jenkins identified them as being identical to those Emile had often received.

"I remember seeing a photograph of a lady lying about his chamber. I asked, 'is that your intended, sir?' He said, 'Perhaps some day.' He told me he was going to be married in March, and he would like me to take him in. There was one time [afterwards when] I said it would be a bad job for him to be ill if he got married, and he said, 'you'll not see that for a long time.'

"I don't recollect any ladies calling on Mr. L'Angelier. One old lady called with her husband, and took tea with him. Sometimes there were messages from other ladies. When he was ill, there was a jar of marmalade sent, and some books, and a card along with it. On the card was 'Mrs. Overton.' "

Prompted by questioning from Moncreiff, Mrs. Jenkins recounted Emile's general health and then related the particulars concerning his three episodes of the stomach illness: "He enjoyed general good health. I recollect his having an illness somewhere about the middle of February. That was not the first serious illness he had had since he came to lodge with me—he had one eight or ten days before."

Regarding the first illness: "One night he wished a pass key, as he thought he would be out late. I knocked at his door about eight [the next] morning, and got no answer. I knocked again, and was answered, 'Come in, if you please.' I went into his room. He said, 'I have been very unwell; look what I have vomited.' I said I thought it was bile. It was a greenish substance. There was a great deal of it. It was thick stuff like gruel. I asked him, 'Why did you not call upon me?' He said that while on the road coming home he was seized with a violent pain in his bowels and stomach, and when he was taking off his clothes he thought he should have died upon the carpet, and no human eye would have seen him. He was not able, he said, to ring the bell. He asked me to make a little tea, and said he would not go out.

"I emptied what he had vomited. I advised him to go to a doctor, and he said he would. He took a little breakfast, and then went to sleep until nine o'clock—about an hour. I went back to him then. He said he was a little better, and he would go out. Mr. Thuau, who lodges in my house, saw him. He rose between ten o'clock and eleven o'clock [saying he would go to his office and would] call on some lady on his way there. After going out, he returned about three in the afternoon. He said he had been at the doctor, and brought a bottle in with him. He took the medicine and complained of being very thirsty. The illness made a great change in his appearance. He looked yellow and dull, and not what he used to be. Before that, his complexion was fresh. He became dark under the eyes, and the red of his cheeks seemed to be more broken. He complained of cold after he came in—of being very cold. He lay down upon the sofa, and I laid a railway rug over him. I did nothing for his feet.

"He never was the same after this illness. He got a little better. When asked how he felt, he was accustomed to say, 'I never feel well.' I have nothing by which to remember the date of this first illness.

"I think the second [illness] was about the 22nd of February. On a Monday morning, about four o'clock, he called me. He was vomiting. It was the same kind of stuff as before, in color and otherwise, but there was not so much of it. He complained on this occasion likewise of pain in the bowels and stomach, and of thirst and cold. I did not know he was out the night before. He did not say anything about it. I put more blankets upon him, put jars of hot water to his feet, and made him tea. I gave him also a great many drinks—toast and water, lemon and water, and such drinks. I called again about six in the morning. He did not rise until the forenoon. He had bought a piece of meat for soup from one Stewart, in St. Georges Road, on Saturday the 21st. He kept a passbook, in which he entered these things. The date of the passbook enables me to remember this. This meat was sent home on the Saturday before this second illness.

"Dr. Thomson came to attend him on Monday. Thuau went for him. It was in the forenoon when the doctor came, but I don't remember the hour. The doctor saw L'Angelier and left a prescription for powders, which I got. L'Angelier was about eight days in the house at that time, away from his office. He took one or two of the powders, but I don't know whether he took the rest. He said they were not doing him the good he expected. He said that the doctor was always saying that he was getting better, but he did not feel well. Dr. Thomson came frequently to see him."

Having covered the first two illnesses, Moncreiff then led the witness through a synopsis of Emile's activities during the final days of his life.

"Sometime after [the second illness], he went to Edinburgh. I don't remember the date of his going. He was, I think, about eight days at Edinburgh. I recollect his coming back—it was, I think, a Tuesday [March 17]. Mr. Thuau told me about four o'clock of the same day that L'Angelier was coming back that evening, and I got some bread and butter for him. He returned that night about half past ten.

"When he came home on March 17, he asked if I had any letter for him. I said, 'no.' He seemed to expect a letter, and to be disappointed at not finding it. He stayed at the time until the 19th.

"Before he went away again, he said that any letters that came were to be given to Mr. Thuau, who would address them. He said he was going to the Bridge of Allan. I don't know if he went anywhere else before going to the Bridge of Allan. He went away about ten in the morning. A letter came for him on the 19th. [This was the letter that later went missing.] It was like the letters which had been in the habit of coming, and I gave it to Mr. Thuau. I don't remember any letters on the Friday, but there was one on the Saturday—more like a lady's handwriting. I also gave this to Mr. Thuau, and he re-addressed them.

"Mr. L'Angelier said he would not be home until Wednesday night or Thursday morning of the following week. He was very much disappointed at not getting a letter before he went away, and he said, 'If I get a letter, perhaps I will be home tonight.'

"I next saw him on Sunday night about eight o'clock. I was surprised to see him so soon. He said the [last] letter . . . had brought him home, and on his asking when it came, I told him that it came on Saturday afternoon. He said he had walked fifteen miles, but did not say where he had come from. He said he intended to leave again the next morning, and desired to be called early. I do not remember whether he said explicitly he was going back to the Bridge of Allan. I think I only understood that.

"He looked much better, and, on being asked, said he was a great deal better and all but well.

"He went out that night about nine o'clock. Before going out, he said, 'If you please, give me the pass key, for I am not sure but I may be late.' He told me to call him early in the morning to go by the first train. He did not say what hour, but I thought it would be between seven and eight o'clock. It was about half past two in the morning, as far as I can remember, when I next saw him."

At this point in her testimony, she described Emile's final hours—from her frequent attempts to nurse him and his request for Mary Perry, to Dr. Steven's pronouncing him dead. She was then asked if she had told everything that she remembered regarding Emile's final hours.

"All I can remember. I did not ask him where he had been. I had no reason to know or suspect where he had been.

"[After he was pronounced dead, I] sent my little boy to Mr. Clark, another lodger. Mr. Clark came, and Mr. Chrystal, who keeps a druggist's shop. Mr. Chrystal went into the room and shut his eyes. The body was still lying in the bed. He said he would send to his employers, but Mr. Menzies, the undertaker, came first—then Miss Perry, then Mr. Stevenson, and I think Mr. Thuau came, too, and Dr. Thomson.

"Mr. Stevenson is one of the young men who worked with Mr. L'Angelier. When he came, I told him I wished him to lock up what belonged to L'Angelier, and he did so. The clothes [Emile] took off at night were laid on the sofa. [Stevenson] took a letter out of [Emile's] pocket and some person—I don't remember whom—said this explained all. I saw the letter and said, 'That is the letter that came on Saturday.' Thuau and Stevenson, and I think Mr. Kennedy and Dr. Thomson were there. I can't say whether it was Stevenson or Thuau who said, 'this explains all.' I think it was Stevenson. Stevenson locked up the things.

"At that time, I don't remember anything being said as to having an examination. He was coffined the night he died, and I think they examined the wardrobe that night. But there was no examination of his body [that night]. Until Stevenson locked them up, everything was left as [when] L'Angelier died."

His questioning completed, Moncreiff sat down and John Inglis then cross-examined Mrs. Jenkins on several points, beginning with the date of Emile's first illness: "[The second] illness was on the 22nd of February. There was an illness before that, but I can't say its date—it might be eight or ten days before the illness of 22nd February.

"As to the illness of the 22nd of February, he dined at home on the Sunday. On the Saturday night, he said he did not intend to go out the next day—he said he was not very well. He was taking fresh herring on the Saturday. I thought that was against him. I said I did not think herring was good for him at that time of the year. He made a sauce of vinegar and egg, and I said that was not good for him. He was also, I thought, using too many vegetables. He said when he was at college in France, he used a good many vegetables.

"The morning of his death, I think Miss Perry came that morning about ten. When she came, I asked, 'Are you the intended?' and she said, 'Oh, no, I am only a friend.' When he asked me to send for Miss Perry, I supposed she was his intended. I told her he was dead, and she seemed very sorry. Her grief was very striking—she seemed very much overwhelmed, and cried a great deal. I was surprised at the excess of her grief. I don't recollect if she asked to see the body, but I took her in and showed it to her. When she went into the room, she kissed his forehead several times. She was crying very much. Mr. Scott, the undertaker, was present at this time, and I think my sister also. Miss Perry said how sorry she was for his mother. I don't remember her saying she knew his mother. When I said to Miss Perry how sorry [his fiancée] would be, she said not to say much about it, or anything about it—I don't recollect which.

"Mr. L'Angelier had two wooden writing desks in his room. I did not see the letters taken away—some of the clothes I knew about, but not the letters. I was not in the room when the officers searched his boxes and clothes. They rang the bell, and said they wanted to search the room, and then said, 'That is all that is required.' There were eight bottles in his room after his death. In one there was laudanum, and in another there was something which appeared to be rhubarb. The authorities took the bottles away. I think Mr. Murray was one of the parties who took them, and Mr. Stevenson. I don't recollect when they got them. It was some days after his death. I was in the room when they took them away.

"[During the final illness, when] I asked if he had taken anything which had disagreed with him, I meant had he taken anything at Bridge of Allan which disagreed with him. I did not refer to his taking anything that night. He answered no, he never felt better than when he was at the country. I did not ask him where he had been that last night, because I thought he had been visiting his intended.

"My husband was from home, and only saw him once, at the New Year time."

Mrs. Jenkins was then dismissed and wound her way out of the crowded courtroom. As she would with every witness, Madeleine had watched the landlady's testimony with complete attention, sometimes leaning forward and resting her chin on her hand.

Other landladies would follow Mrs. Jenkins to the stand, including Mrs. Margaret Houston Clark, Emile's landlady when he lived near the Royal Botanic Garden; and Elizabeth Wallace, the landlady of his first Glasgow lodging house.

Clark described Emile as very "steady and temperate," attending church regularly and enjoying good health. He had "a very great horror of taking medicine," and had discussed Madeleine with her, saying that "[there was] an . . . interruption to his intimacy with Miss Smith. It was within two months of his death. He told me that he was afraid they would not get their end accomplished, as Miss Smith's father was putting stronger obstacles in the way than ever. He said nothing further at that time. He afterwards spoke on the subject, and said something to the same effect. He spoke of no coolness between Miss Smith and himself."

Elizabeth Wallace reiterated Emile's aversion to medicine and stated he claimed to have served once as a lieutenant in the navy. She presented a cheerful picture of Emile in the year before he met Madeleine: "He was a well-conducted young man. He kept good hours—he kept no company. One day he came in [and] said that he had met an old sweetheart going on her marriage jaunt. He was very cheerful. He played the guitar in the evenings, and sang occasionally."

Various newspapers carried all the details of the trial, and the *London Times*, which would feature large sections of verbatim testimony, reported on the first day of the trial: "The Court was crowded, and extraordinary interest was excited by the case. The prisoner, a young lady of remarkably prepossessing appearance, took her place at the bar with a firm step and a composed aspect, her self-control never forsaking her for a moment during the day. The prisoner pleaded 'Not Guilty.'

"She entered into the dock with all the buoyancy with which she might have entered the box of a theater. . . . [She is] short of stature and slight form, with features sharp and prominent, and restless and sparkling eyes . . . her perfect self-possession, indeed, could only be accounted for either by a proud conscience of innocence, or by her possessing an almost unparalleled amount of self-control. [Through her veil she] seemed to scan the witnesses with a scrutinizing glance . . . she even smiled with all the air and grace of a young lady in the drawing room, as her agents came forward at intervals to communicate with her."

The *Ayrshire Express* reported: "Madeleine [turned] right round upon the reporters immediately behind her, to see how they get along with the note-taking which is carrying her name and deeds into every British home."

Landladies appeared yet again when Moncreiff addressed Emile's movements in the weeks and hours previous to his death. The landlady of the Edinburgh lodging house where Emile had stayed in mid-March presented brief testimony ("He appeared to be in very good health, but he told me he had been an invalid"), as did the landlady of the Bridge of Allan lodging house from where he hurriedly departed at the summons of Madeleine's final letter: "He seemed to be in good health and spirits, and took his meals well. He left on

Sunday just after two o'clock. I did not hear him say why he left. He had intended to stay longer."

Concerning Emile's March 10–17 trip to Edinburgh, Moncreiff questioned Jane and James Towers, Mary Perry's sister and brother-in-law. Emile had dined with them during that trip and had mentioned to the Towers that he had recently been ill after taking coffee and cocoa, and suspected that he had been poisoned. When James Towers asked who would possibly want to poison him, Emile did not reply. James went on to state: "He was very fond of talking about himself. I thought he was a vain person. There was much vaporing or rash talking on that occasion. I can't say he was a person who spoke much without thinking.

"He did not say from whom he got the cocoa or coffee. He said coffee agreed with him, and that he was in the habit of taking it. He was not surprised at cocoa not agreeing with him, as he was not accustomed to it."

Concentrating fully on Emile's hasty return to Glasgow from Bridge of Allan, Moncreiff called William Fairfoul of the Caledonian Railway to the stand: "I was the guard of the train which left Stirling in the afternoon of the 22nd of March. It left Stirling at half past three. A gentleman, apparently a foreigner, traveled by that train to Glasgow. I did not know his name at the time, but I know it now."

Fairfoul was then shown the ambrotype portrait of Emile that had been confiscated from Madeleine's bedroom: "I recognize this as a likeness of the gentleman. He went in the train from Stirling to Coatbridge, the nearest part to Glasgow. I asked if he wanted a machine, and he said no, he was hungry and wanted to be shown a place where he could get something to eat. He said he was in no hurry to Glasgow, if he got in at night. There was a Mr. Ross, an auctioneer, who came from Stirling. I showed Mr. L'Angelier and Mr. Ross the road to Glasgow, and they started together. I saw him get some roast beef before leaving—he ate it very heartily. I was with him all the time. He took some porter with the beef.

"There were only about eight passengers of all classes in the train. None except Mr. Ross and this gentleman stopped at Coatbridge. I am quite certain of that. I never saw either Ross or L'Angelier before or since, and I did not know their names or anything about them. I was first examined about this matter four or five days after the occurrence. I was told at Greenhill that I was wanted by the Fiscal at Stirling—and I was examined by him.

"The deceased got the food at MacDonald's, at Coatbridge. I saw him take the beef. He ate a good deal—but neither Ross nor I ate."

Thomas Ross, the auctioneer, followed Fairfoul to the stand and spoke at length of his long walk to Glasgow with the foreign gentleman from the train: "I recollect being in Stirling on the 22nd of March, and leaving by the train in the afternoon for Glasgow. I went by the train to Coatbridge. I did not observe a foreign gentleman in the train, but I saw him when he got out. I did not know his name. The guard said he was going to walk to Glasgow, and I was going to do the same. Before starting, he had some roast beef and a small bottle of porter. I saw him take it. We then started for Glasgow, and I think we took a little more than two hours to get there. It was twenty minutes past five when we left, and it was rather more than half past seven when we reached Glasgow. The distance is eight miles. He had a Balmoral bonnet on his head. He walked well, and did not appear tired when he got to Glasgow. He smoked several times on the road. He did not tell me who he was. He appeared in good health and spirits when we parted. We parted at the top of Abercromby Street, Gallowgate. He said he was going to the Great Western Road.

"He said he had come from Alloa that morning, and that he had walked from Alloa to Stirling. He said the distance was eight miles. He said nothing that I remember about the Bridge of Allan. Our conversation was chiefly about local affairs, such as the scenery around us. He did not eat a great deal at Coatbridge. He told me he had presented a check at the bank at Stirling either the day before or some other day, and that they would not cash it—he being a stranger. Abercromby Street is about the middle of the Gallowgate. I was in no house with him on the way from Coatbridge to Glasgow, and in no shop."

The puzzle of Ross's testimony is his companion's statement of coming from Alloa, rather than from Bridge of Allan. The "foreign gentleman" also gave the correct walking distance from Alloa to Stirling, which is significantly different than the distance between Bridge of Allan and Stirling. Emile had never mentioned a side trip to Alloa to anyone, and John Inglis would later suggest that this man who accompanied Mr. Ross was not Emile L'Angelier.

Narrowing in on the final hours of Emile's life, Moncreiff questioned three witnesses, beginning with James Galloway, an acquaintance of Emile's: "I knew Mr. L'Angelier by sight, [and on] March 22, I saw [him] that night about nine o'clock. He was in Sauchiehall Street. He was going east. He was going in the direction of Blythswood Square. He was about four or five minutes walk from Blythswood Square. He was walking rather slowly."

After Galloway saw him, Emile apparently went to pay a call on his friend, Mr. McAlester. Mary Tweedle, a servant at McAlester's lodging house, testified: "I saw Mr. L'Angelier that night at twenty minutes past nine o'clock. He called at the door and asked for Mr. McAlester, but Mr. McAlester was not at home. L'Angelier wore a light topcoat and a Balmoral bonnet. When he found Mr. McAlester was not at home, he halted a moment at the stairhead and then went away. Mr. L'Angelier did not seem much disappointed that McAlester was not at home. When he halted at the stairhead, he seemed as if he would have liked to come in. I did not ask him to come in."

Tweedle concluded her testimony by saying that it was a five-minute walk from McAlester's lodging's to Blythswood Square.

Mary Tweedle is historically the last person to have seen Emile before he appeared on Mrs. Jenkins' doorstep—a full five hours later.

Thomas Kavan, a night constable, patrolled Blythswood Square during March of 1857. Moncreiff began his questioning by showing Kavan the portrait of Emile: "I have seen this face more than once—[but] I did not know his name. I saw him about two months previous to hearing of his death. I saw him in Main Street, as well as I can recollect about eleven, or between ten and eleven. He was standing near a lamp post at the back lane. When I came along the point of the Square, I turned along Main Street, and he said, 'Cold night, policeman. Do you smoke?' I said, 'Yes sir,' and he put his hand in his breast pocket and gave me two cigars and passed on. He was then not more than the breadth of this court from the wall of Mr. Smith's house.

"I saw him again, ten or twelve days after the first time. He was passing along the garden side by the railings on the north side of Blythswood Square, going east towards Regent Street.

"I saw him [a third time] between a fortnight and three weeks previous to the time I was first examined before the Fiscal. He was then at the corner of Regent Street and Main Street, coming towards Blythswood Square. It was early in the night, but I can't positively say when. I should say between nine and ten o'clock. I never saw him again.

"I was on my beat on Sunday evening, March 22. I did not see him that night. I am quite sure of that."

If Kavan's testimony is genuine, and there is no reason to suspect that it is not, Emile did not spend a great deal of time loitering near Blythswood Square on the night of March 22, or else Kavan presumably would have seen him.

Shifting from the topic of Emile's final movements to the theme of his general character and history, Moncreiff called a variety of friends and coworkers to the stand, beginning with William A. Stevenson, Emile's direct supervisor at Huggins & Company. Stevenson had done most of the legwork in collecting Emile's letters and belongings, and admitted that he was "intimate with him [Emile] in business, but not otherwise."

"He was unwell in March and got a leave of absence. I understood he was going to Edinburgh. He afterwards went to the Bridge of Allan. I got a letter from him at the Bridge of Allan. I answered that letter. I recovered that letter, after his death, at the post office at Bridge of Allan. I was sent to Bridge of Allan on Friday the 27th to take possession of Mr. L'Angelier's things.

"I got notice of his death on the 23rd of March, and went on receipt of that intelligence to the French Consul's office. I saw there Mr. Thuau, who told me that L'Angelier's medical attendant was Dr. Thomson, and I sent for him. I saw

L'Angelier's corpse. I was told that Dr. Steven had also attended, so I sent for him. They said that an examination of the body was the only way of explaining his death. There was, at that time, no suspicion about it. I authorized them to make a postmortem examination the following day. In consequence of what I learned at the examination, I informed the Procurator-Fiscal on Tuesday. I saw them commence the postmortem examination.

"I did not expect L'Angelier in Glasgow on that Sunday night—that was inconsistent with his letter to me, which said he would return 'not later than Thursday morning.'

"When I went to his lodgings on the Monday, his clothes were lying on the sofa in his room. I examined them, and found various articles: a comb, tobacco, three finger rings, five shillings, a bunch of keys, and a letter. The letter was in his vest pocket. The letter began: 'Why, my beloved, did you not come to me?' I made some remarks on getting that letter, but I don't exactly recollect what they were. I said the letter explained why he was in Glasgow, and not in Bridge of Allan."

Next, Stevenson was questioned on his handling of the letters and other articles that were key evidence in the trial: "I found a bunch of keys in his pocket, which I took with me, and I kept them. I put them in the possession of Mr. T. Kennedy, our cashier.

"I knew that Mr. L'Angelier had a memorandum book. I remember having it when coming from his lodgings after seeing the body. I got it in his lodgings, but I cannot tell when. I can identify the memorandum book [a pocket notebook] and also the handwriting within. I made the book into a parcel and sealed it up. I subsequently gave it to Police Officer Murray. Not then, but afterwards, it was marked with the label . . . stating that the book was found in a desk at Huggins [which is not where it was actually found]. A few days ago, I wrote to Mr. Hart, the Fiscal, correcting the mistake.

"I think upon the Wednesday morning, the Fiscal requested me to bring some letters to him, and on going into the desk for them I saw [the notebook]. I took some of the letters to [the Fiscal]—I did not take the book. It was not sealed then.

"I had the key of the desk—it was on the bunch I got from his pocket. I was aware that the lock of the desk was in a frail [state, but] I did not know that the back of it was [also] in a frail state. [Emile] had complained to me that lads about the office got into it. When he complained that his desk was in a frail state, I looked at his desk, and saw a book like this lying in it. I never saw him write in the book.

"Between the Monday and the time I signed the label, [the notebook] was opened frequently. I was always present, but there were others looking at the letters: Mr. Kennedy, the cashier; Mr. Wilson, the invoice clerk; and Mr. Miller, one of the warehousemen. There may have been others belonging to the same department, but none who were strangers to the establishment.

"On the Monday, when I found the [notebook], I turned over the pages—I did not take notice of any of the entries. Under the date of the 11th of February I see an entry—that is L'Angelier's handwriting, and the book is in his handwriting from that date onward. I see an entry on Saturday, March 14. That seems to be the last. All the entries from the 11th of February to the 14th of March inclusive are in L'Angelier's handwriting. They are in pencil, and some of them very faint. I was accustomed to see him write in pencil.

"I never made any inventory of the clothes or other things found in his lodgings, or of the letters."

The contents of Emile's notebook were slight, but meaningful. Emile apparently kept a diary for the period of February 11 through March 14, 1857. Among the entries that recorded his various meals and entertainments are these thirteen pertaining to Madeleine:

Wednesday, February 11:	Saw M. at 12 P.M.
Friday, February 13:	Saw Mimi.
Saturday, February 14:	A letter from M.
Monday, February 16:	Wrote M.
Thursday, February 19:	Saw Mimi a few moments. Was very ill during the night.
Friday, February 20:	Passed two pleasant hours with M. in the Drawing Room.
Sunday, February 22:	Saw Mimi in Dining Room. Promised me French Bible. Taken very ill.
Tuesday, February 24:	Wrote M.
Wednesday, February 25:	M. wrote me.
Saturday, February 28:	Mimi wrote me.
Tuesday, March 3:	Mimi wrote. Wrote Mimi. Saw her in S.S.
Wednesday, March 4:	Saw Mimi. Gave her a note and got one from her.
Thursday, March 5:	Saw Mimi. Gave her a note and rec'd. one.

It is easy to understand why John Inglis eventually requested suppression of this notebook from the jury. If the entries are genuine, and if the cryptic *M.* does, indeed, stand for *Madeleine*, then it shows the couple meeting directly before Emile's illnesses on February 19 and 22. And while Madeleine's first documented arsenic purchase on February 21 cannot account for Emile's illness on the 19th, it could certainly be presented by the prosecution as the cause of his illness on the 22nd.

Madeleine's supporters have made much of the fact that she had not purchased arsenic prior to Emile's first illness. This is most likely true, but the Smith household undoubtedly contained various housekeeping and cleaning materials that were poisonous if ingested. The first illness was a minor one, and if Madeleine had decided to kill Emile, she would have seen in this first attempt that she was on the right track and may have then turned toward the idea of more powerful poisons, soon afterward venturing out to make her first arsenic purchase at Murdoch's.

The validity of the notebook has been dismissed by some biographers as Emile's attempt to frame Madeleine for his own suicide, and they claim that the entries are fabrications. It is indeed puzzling that Madeleine never mentioned in her letters to Emile their "two pleasant hours" in the Drawing Room, their meeting in the Dining Room, nor made reference to a French Bible. Not mentioning one of these occurrences might be understandable. But not to speak of *any* of the three, especially the two meetings, is very unlike Madeleine, even allowing for the distraction caused by the escalating Emile/Minnoch dilemma.

It has also been questioned why Emile, a man who had never previously kept a diary, would suddenly be inspired to do so at this particular point of his life.

William Stevenson continued: "I understood that L'Angelier corresponded with a number of parties in the South and in France. I have seen letters addressed to ladies in France and in England. I have heard him speak about parties in England. He was a vain person, vain of his personal appearance, very much so—[but] he never spoke of himself to me as very successful among ladies.

"He was of a rather mercurial disposition—changeable.

"I am not aware what money he had when he went to Bridge of Allan or to Edinburgh."

After a few final questions about his handling of the letters, Stevenson was dismissed. He had not been an entirely amenable witness, at one point stopping the questioning to state: "This morning I saw Mr. Wilson and Mr. Gray, of the Fiscal's office in Glasgow. I told them I was in a most uncomfortable position about this matter—that I had got quite a sufficiency in the Court—and that I wanted to be done with it. That was not in consequence of anything said by those gentlemen, it was because I felt exceedingly uncomfortable and very unwell. I saw them this morning. I don't know whether it was this morning or yesterday afternoon that I said so, but I said so repeatedly."

Thomas Fleming Kennedy, the cashier at Huggins, would be the only other witness from Emile's office to testify at length: "I knew L'Angelier for about four and a half years, during which he was in Huggins's employment. He was in the habit of coming frequently to my house. He was a well-behaved, well-principled, religious young man. I had great regard for him. I had the means of judging of his character and conduct.

"He enjoyed general good health while in our warehouse. I never thought him very strong, [but] he was not off duty from bad health till latterly.

"He spoke before his death of an attachment to Miss Smith. He said very little—and I knew nothing further than that there was an intimacy till shortly before his death. About a fortnight before the 23rd of February, he came to me between ten and eleven in the morning, crying. He said he had received a letter from Miss Smith that morning, asking back her letters, and wishing the correspondence to cease. I understood she had written there was a coolness on the part of both of them. I said, 'You ought to give up the letters and be done with it.' I made the remark that the lady was not worthy of him. He said he would not give up the letters—he said so distinctly, determinedly. He said he was determined to keep them, but he threatened at the same time to show them to her father. I told him he was very foolish, and that he had much better give them up. He said, 'No, I won't. She shall never marry another man as long as I live.' He also said, 'Tom, it is an infatuation—she'll be the death of me.' He was exceedingly excited during the whole time. That was about the last conversation I had with him. The last time I saw him was on the 9th of March, when he left to go to Edinburgh."

The witness was then asked to identify Emile's handwriting in the diary notebook, which had yet to be presented to the jury: "The entries in the notebook [are] in L'Angelier's writing—excepting one on the 14th of March, the last entry. . . . I am not sure that it is *not* his, but I am not sure that it is his. But I never saw that book in L'Angelier's possession."

Two other Huggins employees testified briefly that, at Emile's request, they had addressed envelopes to Madeleine because Emile "said he did not wish his handwriting to be known."

Moncreiff then directed the prosecution's presentation to an examination of Emile's character outside of the workplace. With the assistance of a French-speaking interpreter, Moncreiff questioned Amadee Thuau, Emile's fellow boarder at Mrs. Jenkins's: "I am a clerk in Glasgow, and . . . went to lodge at Mrs. Jenkins's at the end of December. I knew Mr. L'Angelier, who also lived there. We took our meals together in the same room."

Thuau was then shown the ambrotype portrait of Madeleine that Emile had kept in his room: "[That] was the portrait of his intended. I am not sure whether he ever told me her name. I did hear it [eventually], I do not know exactly from whom, but I think it was from the French Consul.

"I was in the habit of speaking with L'Angelier about her. We also spoke about the correspondence. I knew [by] the end of December that he was to marry a young lady. I knew of some letters, but read none of them. In one of the letters about which Mr. L'Angelier spoke to me, the lady claimed back some of her letters. This was a pretty long time ago.

"I am familiar with Blythswood Square in Glasgow—it was a street nearby. [I once went with him there, and] when Mr. L'Angelier got to the house, he made a slight noise on a pane of glass of the window. I was waiting at a short distance. I walked on while L'Angelier delivered the letter. It is the second window from the corner. I have since shown that window to a police officer.

"L'Angelier was sometimes in the habit of going out at night. I knew where he went on these occasions—to his intended's house.

"I recollect one morning finding that he had been out and very ill in the night. I asked whether he had seen the lady—he said that he saw her. I also asked if he had been unwell after seeing her. He said that he was unwell in her presence.

"I recollect a second illness of L'Angelier. I don't think he was out the night before that. I did not ask him any questions. L'Angelier insisted on going for a doctor—for his own doctor. [During his second illness,] I went for Dr. Thomson at L'Angelier's request.

"I think I remember L'Angelier's coming home from Edinburgh. I recollect getting a letter from him. [After that trip,] I remember L'Angelier going to Stirling. Before going he left instructions about his letters. The instructions were only for one day—two days perhaps. Two letters came when he was away. One I sent to Stirling, the other to Bridge of Allan.

"I saw L'Angelier take laudanum four or five times. I once told him that he took too much. He said that he could not sleep and that was why he took it. I do not know when this was. I mean by saying 'he took much laudanum' that he did so when suffering a good deal."

After Thuau had been excused, August de Mean, the Chancellor to the French Consul, was called to the stand: "I was acquainted with the late Mr. L'Angelier for about three years. I think I got accidentally acquainted with him in a house in Glasgow, but I do not recollect.

"I know Miss Smith. I was acquainted with her family. I knew that in 1856 there was a correspondence going on between L'Angelier and Miss Smith. L'Angelier confided to me this circumstance. Mr. Smith had a house at Row, and I lived at Helensburgh. L'Angelier stayed a night or two with me.

"When he asked my advice, I told him that he ought to go to Miss Smith's family and tell them of his attachment. I told him that was the most gentlemanly way. He said that Mr. Smith was opposed to it, and he did not think it was necessary to apply to him—and that Miss Smith had spoken to her father, and that he was opposed to it. That is more than a year ago.

"I remember that L'Angelier came to my office a few weeks before his death and he spoke about Miss Smith. I said that she was to be married to some gentleman, and when I mentioned the public rumors, he said that it was not true—but if it did come true, he had documents in his possession that would be sufficient to forbid the banns. I don't recollect whether he said that Mr. Smith had written to him on the subject of her reported marriage. I did not see him after that.

"I thought, having [previously been courteously] received by Mr. Smith in his house, that after L'Angelier's death I thought it was my duty to mention the fact of the correspondence having been carried on between L'Angelier and his daughter—in order that he should take steps to exonerate his daughter in case of anything coming out. I thought that these letters were love letters, and that it would be much better that they should be in Mr. Smith's hands than in the hands of strangers."

De Mean then recounted his conversation with Madeleine on the day after Emile's death, and also testified that Emile had previously mentioned suffering from two attacks of cholera: "I once heard him speak of arsenic, it must have been in the winter of 1854. It was on a Sunday, but I don't recollect how the conversation arose. It lasted about half an hour. Its purport was: how much arsenic a person could take without being injured by it. He maintained it was impossible to [harm oneself] by taking small quantities.

"L'Angelier once stated to me that he had been jilted by an English lady, a rich person, and he said that, on account of that deception, he was almost mad for a fortnight and ran about, getting food from a farmer in the country. He was easily excited. When he had any cause of grief, he was affected very much.

"After my marriage, I had little intercourse with L'Angelier. I thought that he might be led to take some harsh steps in regard to Miss Smith, and as I had some young ladies in my house, I did not think it was proper to have the same intercourse with him as when I was a bachelor. By *harsh*, I mean rash. I was afraid of an elopement with Miss Smith. There had been a long cessation of [my] intercourse with him before he came to me a short time before his death."

The Lord Justice-Clerk then asked for de Mean's general opinion of the dead man: "My opinion of L'Angelier's character at the moment of his death was that he was a most regular young man in his conduct . . . religious . . . and in fact he was most exemplary in all his conduct. The only objection I heard made to him was that he was vain and a boaster, boasting of grand persons whom he knew. For example, when he spoke of Miss Smith he would say: 'I shall forbid Madeleine to do such a thing, or such another thing. She shall not dance with such a one or such another.' "

Emile did not, de Mean testified, boast of his success with females; and when asked if Emile was jealous of Madeleine's paying attention to other men, de Mean replied, "No. [He was jealous] of others paying attentions to Miss Smith."

A witness eagerly anticipated by the courtroom's audience took the stand late in the afternoon of July 3. Mary Arthur Perry was described by a reporter as "a little old maid, in quiet black bonnet and brown dress . . . and a pair of spectacles imparting quaintness to her face."

"I was acquainted with the late Mr. L'Angelier. I became acquainted with him about the year 1853. We both attended the same chapel, St. Jude's. I was first introduced to him by a lady now resident in England, Miss Philpot. I knew his mother lived in Jersey. I never inquired what her occupation was. He had two sisters, and he had a brother who died some time before. I don't know that I ever inquired what his occupation was.

"Latterly, we addressed each other by our Christian names. I addressed him by his surname, and he addressed me *Dear Mary*, or *My dear Mary*. Never *Dearest Mary*.

"In the early part of the summer of [1855] he told me he was engaged to Miss Madeleine Smith—and I was aware from him, from that time forward, of the progress of his attachment and correspondence. Mr. L'Angelier told me he was introduced to Miss Smith at a lady's house—at Mrs. Baird's. He said he had met her there.

"In August of 1855, I was introduced to Miss Smith—he brought her to call on me. When she was introduced to me, I knew the engagement had existed for a few weeks, but I don't know how long they had been intimate with each other. After that, I received several letters from her.

"I was not at all acquainted with [the] Smith family. When L'Angelier brought Miss Smith to see me, I knew the correspondence was clandestine. He told me that when the first engagement was formed he wished to tell her father, but she objected. He then asked her to tell her father herself, but she objected to that also, and he was very much distressed. I knew that he was not acquainted with her father or mother, but he knew her sister.

"I was aware that their intimacy was disapproved of by the family, and that the engagement was broken off at one time. In one of the notes she wrote me, she says her mother had become aware of it. I never knew that her father or mother had abated their dislike of the intimacy. I wrote on one occasion to Miss Smith advising her to mention it to her parents. I advised L'Angelier not to renew the engagement after it was broken till her parents were aware of it. I knew that they met clandestinely. I corresponded with both at the time.

"L'Angelier was frequently at my house, and dined with me occasionally. Down to the beginning of February 1857, he had generally good health, but during that February he seemed not so well as formerly.

"In the beginning of [that month], he said he had heard a report of another gentleman paying attentions to Miss Smith. He said Miss Smith had written him on the subject. One time she had denied it, and another time she had evaded the question.

"He dined with me on Tuesday, the 17th of February. He told me that day when he next expected to see her—that was to be on Thursday [the 19th]. I did not see him again till the 2nd of March. He was looking extremely ill then. When he came in he said: 'Well, I never expected to have seen you again. I was so ill.' He said he had fallen on the floor and been unable to ring the bell. He said he could not attribute his illness to any cause. He did not say what day [his illness] was; but from circumstances, I knew it was the 19th of February. He did not tell me he had seen Miss Smith on the 19th, [but] told me of having had a cup of chocolate which had made him ill.

"On the 9th of March, he took tea with me [and] said: 'I can't think why I was so unwell after getting that coffee or chocolate from her.' I understood he referred to two different occasions—and *her* meant Miss Smith. He was talking about her at the time. He did not say that the severe illness which came on after the coffee or chocolate was the [same] illness he had referred to on the 2nd of March—but I understood so. On the 9th of March, he was talking of his extreme attachment to Miss Smith. He spoke of it as a fascination. He said: 'It's a perfect fascination—my attachment to that girl. If she were to poison me, I would forgive her.' I said: 'You ought not to allow such thoughts to pass through your mind. What motive could she have for giving you anything to injure you?' He said: 'I don't know that, perhaps she might not be sorry to be rid of me.' All this was said in earnest, but I interpreted the expression 'to be rid of me' to mean rid of her engagement. From what he said, there seemed to be some suspicion in his mind as to what Miss Smith had given him, but it was not a serious suspicion.

"He spoke of her intended marriage [to Minnoch]. He said he had heard she was to be married, but he said he had offered to her some months before to discontinue the engagement, but she would not then have it broken. Some time afterwards she wished him to return her letters, and she would return his. He refused to do this, but offered to return the letters to her father. That is what he told me. I did not understand the meaning to be that he threatened to show the letters to her father. I understood that to be a consent on his part to give up the engagement, and he so represented it. Miss Smith would not accede to that proposal, and the engagement remained unbroken at Miss Smith's desire.

"I never saw him again alive.

"Letter No. 141 is a letter from Mr. L'Angelier to me. It is dated Bridge of Allan, March 20. The last paragraph is: 'I should have come to see someone last night, but the letter came too late, so we are both disappointed.' I understood that the paragraph referred to Miss Smith.

"On the 23rd of March I received a message: 'Mr. L'Angelier's compliments—he was very ill at Franklin Place and would be very glad if I would call.' That was about ten in the morning. I went about midday and found he was dead.

"I called on Mrs. Smith and intimated his death to her. I saw Miss Madeleine Smith, but I did not mention it to her. She recognized me and shook hands and asked me to go into the drawing room, and asked if I wished to see her Mama. She also asked if anything was wrong. I said I wanted to see her Mama, and that I would acquaint her with the object of my visit. I did not know Mrs. Smith before."

Miss Perry concluded: "I had a warm affection for Mr. L'Angelier and corresponded with him frequently. I thought him a strictly moral and religious man. He was a regular attendant at church. I was very much agitated by the sudden shock of hearing of his death. I saw the body, and was very much shocked."

Unknowingly, Mary Perry had provided the defense with a crucial piece of their case: uncertainty as to the date of Emile's first illness. Perry was positive that it had occurred on the 19th of February, but Mrs. Jenkins's testimony placed it much earlier, "eight to ten days before the [second] illness of 22nd February." The defense would make much of this discrepancy in their presentation.

The *London Times* continued to report on Madeleine's hearty demeanor: "[Madeleine] entered the Court in her usual airy manner, and sat for some time unveiled; she appeared in excellent health, and never during the day even slightly hung her head, except when reference was made to her love letters with the deceased."

Temporarily leaving personal themes for the more scientific, Moncreiff divided the complex medical evidence into two separate areas: Emile's general health (which had been touched on by other witnesses), and the postmortems performed on his remains.

The first witness of this phase was Emile's general physician, Dr. Hugh Thomson, who was called to the stand the morning of July 1: "I knew the late Mr. L'Angelier for fully two years. He consulted me professionally—the first time fully a year ago."

Regarding the second illness: "I saw him again on the 23rd of February. He was very feverish, and his tongue was furred and had a patchy appearance, from the fur being off in various places. He complained of nausea, and said he had been vomiting. He was prostrate, his pulse was quick, and he had the general symptoms of fever. I prescribed for him. I took his complaint to be a bilious derangement, and I prescribed an aperient draught. He had been unwell, I think, for a day or two—but he had taken worse the night before he called on me. It was during the night of the 22nd and morning of the 23rd that he was taken worse. He was confined to the house for two or three days afterwards. I visited him on the 24th, 25th, and 26th of February. On the 26th he felt considerably better and cooler, and I did not think it necessary to repeat my visits till I happened to be in the neighborhood. On March 1, I intended to visit him, but I met him [unexpectedly] on the Great Western Road."

When questioned about the specific medications he had prescribed for Emile, Thomson stated: "The aperient draught . . . on the 23rd contained magnesia and soda. On the 24th, I prescribed some powders containing rhubarb, soda, chalk of chamomile, and ipecacuanha.

"It did not occur to me at the time that these symptoms arose from the action of any irritant poison; [but] if I had known he had taken an irritant poison, these were the symptoms which I should have expected to follow. I don't think I asked him when he was first taken ill. I had not seen him for some little time before, and certainly he looked very dejected and ill. His color was rather darker and jaundiced—and around the eye, the color was rather darker than usual. . . . About the 26th of February, I think, I told him to give up smoking—I thought that was injurious to his stomach.

"I saw him again eight or ten days after the 1st of March. He called on me, and I have no note of the day. He was then much the same as on the 1st of March. He said that he was thinking of going to the country, but he did not say where. I did not prescribe medicines for him then. . . . I never saw him again in life.

"On the morning of March 23, Mr. Stevenson and Mr. Thuau called on me and mentioned that Mr. L'Angelier was dead, and they wished me to go and see the body, and see if I could give any opinion as to the cause of death. They did not know that I had seen him alive during his last illness. I went to the house. The body was laid out on a stretcher lying on the table. The skin had a slightly jaundiced hue. I said it was impossible to give any decided opinion as to the cause of death, and I requested Dr. Steven to be called, who had been in attendance. I examined the body with my hands externally, and over the region of the liver, the sound was dull—the region seemed full—and over the region of the heart the sound was natural. I saw what he had vomited, and I made inquiry as to the symptoms before death. When Dr. Steven arrived, he corroborated the landlady's statements as far as he was concerned.

"On the afternoon of Monday, I was called on by Mr. Huggins and another gentleman, and I said the symptoms were such as might have been produced by an irritant poison. I said . . . that if it had occurred in England, a coroner's inquest would be held. The next morning, Mr. Stevenson called again and said that Mr. Huggins requested me to make an inspection. In consequence of that,

I said I would require a colleague, and Dr. Steven was agreed on. I called on him, and he went with me to the house, and we made the inspection on Tuesday forenoon. We wrote a short report of that examination for Mr. Huggins immediately. We later made an enlarged report [which discerned nothing remarkable externally and found generally healthy internal organs]."

Inside the stomach was "about half a pint of dark fluid resembling coffee which was poured into a bottle and the stomach preserved." The cause of death was determined to be "either poison or the effect of exposure to cold after much bodily fatigue, which we understand the deceased to have undergone." The stomach, Thomson testified, was sent to Dr. Penny for further examination.

"On the 31st of March, I received instructions from the Procurator-Fiscal to attend at the Ramshorn Church, by order of the Sheriff, to make an inspection of L'Angelier's body. Dr. Steven, Dr. Corbet, and Dr. Penny were there. The coffin was in a vault, and was opened in our presence and the body taken out. I recognized it as L'Angelier's body. It presented much the same appearance as when we left it—it was particularly well-preserved, considering the time that had elapsed. On that occasion, we removed [sections of the colon, intestine, liver, and brain] for analysis [by Dr. Penny]."

During the postmortem, "small whitish and somewhat gritty particles" were found in the intestines and bowels.

Complete written reports of both autopsies were then presented to the court, and Dr. Thomson was excused.

Dr. James Steven, the physician who had attended Emile during his final hours, followed Dr. Thomson to the stand. He verified Dr. Thomson's medical testimony, and his details of Emile's last hours were virtually identical to those given by Mrs. Jenkins.

Dr. Frederick Penny, the professor of Chemistry at Andersonian University, reported finding eighty-two grains of arsenic during his examination of Emile's stomach and its contents—almost one-fifth of an ounce. He further determined: "that the quantity of arsenic found was considerably more than sufficient . . . four or six grains are generally regarded as sufficient to destroy life. Arsenic is an irritant poison. It is absorbed into the blood and through the blood it reaches all the organs in which we find it."

Dr. Penny also testified that he had independently purchased and examined arsenic from both Murdoch's and Currie's, and found them to be roughly 95 percent arsenic and 5 percent coloring matter. He stated he had "no difficulty" in detecting the coloring matter in the stomachs of dogs that had ingested the two arsenic samples. His analysis of the bottles taken from Emile's lodgings found medicine and colognes, but no arsenic.

When asked about the cosmetic uses of poisons, he stated: "I never heard of prussic acid being used externally as a cosmetic—I should think it highly dangerous to use it in that way. I should say it would be very dangerous to use arsenic for a similar purpose. There are cases in which it has been applied to the entire or whole skin and in which the symptoms of poisoning have been produced: vomiting, pain, but not death. I have heard of it being used as a depilatory, to remove hairs from the skin, [but it is] mixed [then] . . . with other matters, lime generally, and solid.

"If the arsenic were given with solid food, and in a solid state, a large portion of the arsenic would be ejected if all that food were vomited. But if the arsenic were stirred up with a liquid, I would not expect that so considerable a portion would be ejected by vomiting.

"There are cases on record in which very large quantities of arsenic have been found in the stomach and intestines, [but] did not turn out to be cases of intentional murder, [but was] taken by the party voluntarily with the intention to commit suicide. It would be very difficult to covertly give a large dose of arsenic in a liquid—by a large dose of arsenic, you exclude many vehicles in which arsenic might be administered. Cocoa or coffee is a vehicle in which a large dose might be given.

"[But] there is a great difference between giving rise to suspicion and actual detection. I have found, by actual experiment, that when thirty or forty grains of arsenic are put into a cup of warm chocolate, a large portion of the arsenic settles down in the bottom of the cup, and I think a person drinking such poisonous chocolate would suspect something when the gritty particles came into his mouth. But if the same quantity, and even a larger quantity, was *boiled with* the chocolate, instead of merely being stirred or mixed, none of it settles down. Coffee or tea could not be made the vehicle of a very large dose of arsenic [in this manner of boiling—but chocolate could]."

Dr. Robert Christison, the next witness, performed an analysis on nine portions of Emile's cadaver that had been sent to him by Dr. Penny. Christison verified the presence of arsenic in all of the samples, and stated that although it would be difficult to remove the coloring matter from arsenic, it could be accomplished by washing the powder with cold water: "I was not asked to attend to the coloring matter. I did not see it, and I did not search for it. Supposing soot or indigo to have been administered with the arsenic, I think it might have been found in the intestines by casual examination—but I cannot say it would have been found. Many of the component parts of soot are insoluble, and it might have been partially removed by frequent vomiting.

"If there was great vomiting and purging, the quantity of arsenic administered must have been much greater than what was found in his stomach and intestines, [maybe] four or five times as much. The time between which the poison is administered and the manifestation of symptoms is about two hours. I had a case lately in which it was five hours. There are also cases in which it was seven and even ten hours. It does not appear that the size of the dose affects this—more important is how the arsenic is administered.

"Active exercise would hasten the effects of arsenic. A long walk would do so. That a man should take poison at Bridge of Allan [and then] come to Coatbridge, walk eight miles to Glasgow, and reach Glasgow in good health and spirits, I should think very unlikely."

Dr. Christison concluded his testimony by recalling unusual research he had performed: "There has been a great dispute as to whether arsenic has taste, and after the strong observations which are published on the subject, a much greater authority than myself, Professor Orfila, still adhered to the opinion that it is acrid. All I can say on the subject is, that experiments were made by myself and two others—as far as it was possible to make experiments with so dangerous a substance—and we found that the taste was very slight indeed. If anything, [it was] sweetish, but all but imperceptible . . . if there is anything perceptible in the taste, it is not such that it could be detected in cocoa or coffee. We all tasted it both in the solid and liquid state, and we held it as far back along the tongue as we could do with safety so as to enable us to spit it out afterwards. We allowed it to remain a couple of minutes and then spat it out, and washed the mouth carefully. Professor Orfila of Paris still maintains that it has an acrid taste. But I think I should add it has always struck me as very strange that neither Orfila, nor any others who doubted my observations, have actually made the experiments themselves."

After concluding the medical evidence presentation, Moncreiff approached the topic of the Smith household by introducing evidence about the house itself: a floor plan of the Blythswood Square home drawn by a civil engineer/architect. The prosecution hoped to illustrate how Madeleine could have secretly brought Emile into that house, and thereby challenge her earlier statement that he had never been inside.

The floor plan was missing key information regarding windowsills and the height of the walls surrounding the house, however, which caused the Lord Justice-Clerk to dismiss the man with the remark: "You might [as well have not] made a plan at all, sir."

The civil engineer's brief appearance was followed by the presentation of Madeleine's Declaration to the court, and she reportedly showed no emotion when its contents were read aloud.

The first witness to answer questions concerning the Smith family household was William Murray, the houseboy whom Madeleine had sent to obtain the prussic acid. His testimony illustrated how unconcerned the servants could be about security and the whereabouts of house keys, and thus showed how easily a secret visitor could have been slipped inside.

"I was a servant with Mr. Smith in Blythswood Square [and] went to his service at the November term. I slept in the room [downstairs and across the hall from Madeleine's room]. Miss Madeleine and Miss Janet sometimes got hot water before going to bed. They got it from the kitchen in a jug, not in a kettle. [Their] room has two windows [onto] Main Street.

"[The servants] in the house, besides me, [were] a cook and a housemaid, Charlotte MacLean and Christina Haggart. They slept [downstairs] in the room at the other end of the passage from the kitchen, close by the back door.

"I never heard of Mr. L'Angelier's death till I was examined by the Procurator-Fiscal. I did not know Mr. L'Angelier by sight. I have posted letters for Miss Smith. I have observed some letters with an address like 'L'Angelier,' but I could not make out what it was."

After recalling the incident regarding the prussic acid, young Murray recounted the Smith household's activities on the night of Sunday, March 22: "On the evening of the 22nd, Christina Haggart was ill. She kept her bed till about six o'clock that evening. [By nine,] all the family and servants were at prayers. Miss Madeleine was there also. Nine o'clock is the usual hour for prayer, and they were about the usual hour that night. When I came downstairs after prayers, I went into the kitchen and stopped five minutes, and then I went to bed . . . at ten, or thereabouts. I slept very soundly. I heard no noise before the morning. Miss Madeleine had not gone to her room before I went to bed.

"I served at breakfast next morning as usual. Miss Smith was there as usual. At this time a young man named MacKenzie, who was visiting Christina Haggart [was there]. She is married to him now."

Murray was then questioned about the various doors and gates of the Blythswood Square home, and his response showed negligent security at every entrance. Murray was responsible for locking the front gate of the fence surrounding the house, but "sometimes I forgot to do it." There were two keys to this front gate, one was kept in Murray's room and the other "hung on a nail in the kitchen. Very seldom both were in the kitchen." Christina Haggart had responsibility for the key to the back gate of the perimeter fence, although Murray stated "any person could have gotten it." The key to the back door, Haggart would later testify, "always stood in the door—on the inside," and the back gate itself "was sometimes locked, but generally unlocked." The keys to the side door and front door of the house were "generally left in the door." The perimeter of the house was a fence, Murray said, "about six feet high and there is broken glass on the top of it," although Christina Haggart would later state that "it is more than six feet high—it may be twelve feet high."

Questioned about Madeleine's flight to Row, Murray said: "I recollect Miss Madeleine being missed from home one morning—[about] six weeks or two months [after] she asked me to go to the apothecary's. The day that she was missing was on the Thursday after the 22nd of March. I heard about ten o'clock [in the morning] that she had gone away. Mrs. Smith told me. Miss Madeleine came back that night."

Christina (Haggart) MacKenzie was called to the stand on July 2. The Smith family's former housemaid would give the courtroom spectators the most intimate glimpse of life within the Smith household, and would supply the most damaging evidence against Madeleine.

"I was a servant in the family of Mr. Smith, Miss Smith's father. I was two years there. I left at last Whitsunday. The family consisted of Mr. and Mrs. Smith and five children. Mr. Smith has a house at Rowaleyn, near Row. They lived there during the summer. They went about May and came back about November. During the first winter I was with them, they lived in India Street, Glasgow. That was the winter before last. Last winter they stayed at 7 Blythswood Square. While they lived in India Street, Miss Smith pointed out a French gentleman to me. She did not speak of him by his name; I came to know his name when I was examined at the County Buildings. The name was L'Angelier. Miss Smith, when she pointed him out, told me he was a friend of hers. He was in the street when she pointed him out, and we were in the drawing room. He was passing."

Christina was then shown Emile's portrait: "That is a likeness of him. I heard that Miss Smith was to be married shortly before her apprehension. Mrs. Smith told me of it. I don't remember the time—it was a good deal before her apprehension. In consequence of that, I asked Miss Smith what she was to do with her other friend, [the French gentleman], and she told me then or sometime after that she had given him up. I asked if she had got back her letters. She said no, that she did not care."

When questioned about Madeleine's stated use of arsenic, Christina testified: "I had charge of cleaning out Miss Smith's bedroom. During February or March, I never observed that the water in her basin was colored peculiarly black or peculiarly blue. I saw nothing unusual of that sort—and I never saw any rats in the house in Blythswood Square. We were not troubled with rats."

Christina also testified about her crucial role in the covert exchange of letters between Madeleine and Emile: "Letters came to me intended for Miss Smith while we lived in India Street. Miss Smith said they would be so addressed. She said they were from her friend. I thought she meant L'Angelier. I can't say how many letters came so addressed. A good many came to India Street, and I gave them all to Miss Smith. Letters also came to Rowaleyn addressed to me for Miss Smith, but there were very few. I called for letters addressed to Miss Bruce at the Post Office in Row. Miss Smith asked me to call for them, and I got them and gave them to Miss Smith. She has given me letters to post for her, addressed to L'Angelier. I posted letters for her with [his] address, in India Street, in Blythswood Square, and during the two summers I was at Rowaleyn. After I had received some letters for Miss Smith, I declined to take more. The reason was that her mother had found fault with me for taking them, and had forbidden me to take them. I was desired by Mrs. Smith not to receive letters—but I did receive some afterwards. I have [hand delivered] a letter with that address in Franklin Place. I only delivered one letter so addressed—I left it at the house."

Recalling March 22, the night of Emile's poisoning, Christina stated: "I was not well that day, and kept my bed in consequence. I got up between five and six o'clock in the afternoon. I saw my present husband [Duncan MacKenzie] that evening. He came between seven and eight o'clock. [He] was frequently in the house at that time—several times in the course of a week.

"There was family worship that evening at nine o'clock. I was present. Miss Smith was present, and the rest of the family. MacKenzie remained in the house when I went up to family worship, and he was there when I came down. I left Miss Smith in the dining room when I came down, and I did not see her that evening. I went to bed at ten o'clock. The cook slept with me as usual that night. MacKenzie left near ten, or thereabouts. I was not aware of anything taking place in the house during the night. I did not hear anything, and was not aware of any stranger being [inside]. When MacKenzie went away, I saw him to the back door and the outer gate. I snibbed [latched] the gate, and I have no reason to suppose I did not lock the inner back door as usual. I left Miss Smith in the dining room with the rest of the family after prayers. I did not see her again that night. She gave me no reason to suppose she had any meeting that night."

Of Madeleine's sudden flight to Row, Christina remembered little: "I remember Miss Smith leaving home suddenly on the Thursday after that Sunday. One evening that week Miss Smith was out at an evening party. I could not say if she was home at the usual time on the Wednesday evening. On Thursday morning it was discovered that Miss Smith was not at home. I don't know if it was found she had taken any of her clothes with her. I saw her on her return. A small carpet bag, containing things of hers, was brought back with her. The bag was not *very* small."

In respect to Madeleine and Emile's meetings, Christina denied any knowledge of such encounters at the summer home ("when the family were at Rowaleyn, I don't recollect seeing him there or in the neighborhood"), but presented detailed information about trysts in both Glasgow houses.

"I have seen him [inside] the house in India Street. I was asked once by Miss Smith to open the back gate to let him in, and I did so. This was during the day—I think they were all at church except the youngest sister, Janet. It was on a Sunday. Miss Smith went in with him to the laundry. The door was shut when they went in. I don't remember how long he remained—I think about a half hour.

"He came back to the house at night oftener than once. I don't think more than three or four times. He came about ten o'clock, before the family retired to their rooms. As far as I remember, they were all at home. On these occasions, he stood at the back gate. He did not, to my knowledge, come into the house. I don't know if he came in. I opened the back gate to him by Miss Smith's directions. She asked me to open the door for her friend. On some occasions when I went to open the gate he was there, and on others he was not. I did not see Miss Smith go out to him. I left open the back door of the house leading to the gate. There was no person in the laundry at the time—the back door was a good piece away from the laundry. Miss Smith and this gentleman might have gone into the laundry without me seeing them. During the season we lived in India Street, I pointed out this gentleman to Duncan MacKenzie, my present husband. I said he was a friend of Miss Smith's. I have spoken to that gentleman during the season we were in India Street. He made me a present of a dress. He did not say what he gave it for."

On the topic of meetings within the Blythswood Square home, which Madeleine told de Mean had never occurred, Christina remembered one episode in particular: "In the Blythswood Square house, there was a back door leading to an area and into a lane. [Miss Smith] asked me once to open it for her. I don't know when that was—it was a good long time before Miss Smith was apprehended. I don't recall whether it was two months before—it might be about two months. It was at night, I think past ten, that she asked me to open the door. I was in her room when she asked me to do this. Her room was downstairs, on the same floor as the kitchen. Her youngest sister slept with Miss Smith, and she was in bed by that time. I slept in a back room near to the back door. The cook, Charlotte McLean, slept with me. At the time I speak of, Charlotte McLean was in the kitchen. I opened the back gate into the lane. I saw no person there, [but] I have seen L'Angelier in Main Street [on another occasion], close to the [Blythswood] house, at night. He was walking slowly.

"[This particular night,] I left [the back gate and back door] open and returned to the house. Miss Smith [had] asked if I would open the back door and stay in the kitchen a little, because she was to see her friend. She did not say where she was to see the friend. Miss Smith met me in the passage, she was going towards the back door. I heard footsteps coming through the gate. I did not hear where Miss Smith went to. I did not hear the door of my room shut. I don't know how long [Charlotte McLean and] I remained in the kitchen. I think it would be more than half an hour. While I stayed in the kitchen, I did not know where Miss Smith was. I did not know that she was in my bedroom. I had no doubt that she *was* there, but I did not know it, [although] the interview between Miss Smith and he *might* take place in the lobby. When we heard Miss Smith go to her room, I left the kitchen. We heard the door of Miss Smith's bedroom shut—I did not hear the back door of our house shut. I am not certain, but I think I found it shut when I went to my bedroom."

When asked about the possibility of Madeleine and Emile meeting without her knowledge, Christina testified: "At night, when we were in bed, Miss Smith could have passed from her bedroom to the kitchen, or upstairs, without being overheard by me. The stair leading up to the dining room floor is very near her bedroom door. The back door makes a noise in opening [and undoing] the lock makes a considerable noise. It is close to my bedroom. [But] a person [inside the house] could open the back door by the key in the door, and open the gate in the wall by unsnibbing [unlatching] it."

Christina was then excused from the stand. By stating that Madeleine *had* met Emile at least once inside the Blythswood house, and outlining how easily Madeleine could have brought Emile undetected into that house on other occasions, Christina had strongly damaged the defense's case.

Duncan MacKenzie, Christina Haggart's new husband, was questioned soon after his wife. His testimony sadly illustrated that Madeleine believed all men behaved as irrationally as Emile did: "One night, I was coming up to the India Street house and saw L'Angelier standing. He asked me if I was going into the house, and I said I was. He asked me if I knew Christina, and he asked me if I would ask her to come out and speak to him. I did so, and she went out to speak to him. I was present when they met, but I did not hear what was said. I saw them talking together. I was not jealous about them. Christina was afraid I might be. I later had a letter signed 'M. Smith' saying it was *her* friend that I had seen, and therefore she hoped nothing would arise between Christina and me. I never saw the gentleman again. I was frequently about that house and the house in Blythswood Square after that."

Narrowing in scope from the Smith household to Madeleine in particular, Moncreiff brought several witnesses to the stand, beginning with Mary Jane Buchanan, the friend who had accompanied Madeleine on her March 6 arsenic purchase. This witness reportedly "wept bitterly" throughout her testimony: "I was at school with Miss Smith . . . near London. She came after I was there two years, and I think she was there a year with me. I have been acquainted with her ever since.

"One day last spring, [Madeleine and] I went into a chemist's shop in Sauchiehall Street. It was Currie's shop. I don't remember if she told me what she was going in for."

Buchanan then related the details of the arsenic purchase to the jury.

"Leaving the shop, I laughed at the idea of a young lady buying arsenic—she said nothing, but laughed too.

"I have frequently seen her write and am well acquainted with her handwriting. I have been shown by the Procurator-Fiscal a number of letters, and I examined them carefully with the view of ascertaining if they were in her handwriting—and I came to the conclusion that they were.

"In the course of last spring, she wrote to me, telling me she was engaged to be married—that was in the very end of February. She said she was engaged to Mr. Minnoch. She afterwards spoke to me on the subject on the 6th and 31st of March. On both these occasions she spoke of herself as engaged to be married to Mr. Minnoch, and of the marriage as likely to take place in June. She spoke of no doubt or difficulty about it at all.

"When we were at school . . . I remember, either in a lesson or . . . I think it was in the course of reading in the evenings, that an account was given of Styrian peasants taking arsenic to give them breath to climb steep hills, and about their having a peculiar plumpness and rosiness of complexion.

"I remember a Miss Guibilei. She was a pupil-teacher. She gave her services as a teacher of music in exchange for being taught other things herself. She was there, I think, at the time of the reading in question. I suppose Miss Smith was there. I don't remember, but we were always obliged to be present at these readings, and so I should think Miss Smith was there."

The next witness was the pupil-teacher herself, Augusta (Guibilei) Walcot: "I was a pupil-teacher at [the] school . . . at which Miss Smith was, in the year of 1852. I never advised her to use arsenic as a cosmetic, or to apply it to her face, neck or arms mixed with water, nor to use it in any way. I had no conversation with her, that I recollect of, about the use of arsenic. I believe I had no conversation with her about the use of cosmetics in their external application to the skin.

"I recollect one evening, in the course of reading, it was mentioned that Swiss mountaineers took arsenic to improve their breathing in ascending hills, and that those who took it were remarkable for plumpness and a general appearance of good health. I believe I had no conversation with Miss Smith about this passage."

Mrs. Walcot's testimony, by directly contradicting Madeleine's Declaration, further damaged the defense's case.

On July 2, the courtroom spectators were rewarded with the appearance of William Minnoch. Minnoch had learned the depth of Madeleine's involvement with Emile only after her arrest. He would never have the opportunity to speak with her privately about the matter—in fact, they would never speak again. Their engagement was canceled, probably through private conversations between Minnoch and Madeleine's father, although the details of the dissolution are not known. Madeleine reportedly leaned forward attentively during Minnoch's entire testimony, interested in every word. A reporter at the trial described this witness as "a man of apparently thirty-five years, though a fair complexion makes him look younger. He is short and slim, perhaps one of the best-dressed men . . . with a keen-cut and more ladylike face than that of the woman to whom he was betrothed."

"I am a merchant in Glasgow," Minnoch began, "and a partner of the firm of John Houldsworth and Company. I live in Main Street, above the house of Mr. James Smith. I have been intimately acquainted with his family for upwards of four years. In the course of last winter I paid my addresses to Miss Madeleine Smith, and I made a proposal of marriage to her [and she] accepted me on the 28th of January—and we arranged it more particularly on the 12th of March. The marriage was fixed to be on the 18th of June. From the 28th of January to the end of March, there was nothing which suggested any doubt to my mind as to the engagement continuing. I had no idea she was engaged to any other person, and I was aware of no attachment or peculiar intimacy between her and any other man.

"I [once] made Miss Smith a present of a necklace—it was sometime in January, before the 28th."

John Inglis asked Minnoch about his actions on the night of February 19, the possible date of Emile's first illness: "I was at the opera on that night. I was accompanied by my sister and Miss Smith. [One of Madeleine's biographers states the opera was, perhaps fittingly, *Lucretia Borgia*.] My sister and myself called for Miss Smith. We went to the opera about half past seven o'clock. We got home about eleven o'clock. Miss Smith returned with us. She had been with us all evening. The cab stopped at her door, and she went into her house. I did not observe who received her on that occasion—somebody opened the door."

Minnoch then related what he knew of Madeleine's activities during the month of March: "She went along with her family to the Bridge of Allan on the 6th of March. She remained there till the 17th. I visited the family while they were there. After leaving, I received a letter from Miss Smith.

"After she came home from Bridge of Allan, she dined in my house with her father and mother. That was on March 19.

"On the 25th, I called for Mr. Smith, but I did not see him. He was unwell and in bed. [That night] I took Miss Smith to [a dinner at] Mr. Middleton's. He is the minister of the church they attend. I was not aware of anything wrong at that time.

"I called on Thursday morning, the 26th, at her father's house. She was not in the house—I was informed she had left the house."

At this point, Minnoch recalled his hasty trip with Madeleine's brother, Jack; their finding her on the steamer going to Helensburgh; and the threesome's eventual return to Glasgow.

"I saw her again on the Saturday following, the 28th of March. I had heard a rumor that something was wrong. I reminded her of the promise she made to me at Row that she would 'tell me by and by.' I had not heard anything of L'Angelier then—she [had] not [mentioned] his name. I think she [had previously] said she had written to a Frenchman to get back her letters. I did not know who the Frenchman was. [That Saturday morning,] she told me that she had written to Mr. L'Angelier. She made no further statement at that time.

"I saw her again on the Sunday—there was no conversation on the subject then.

"I saw her on Monday and Tuesday. On Tuesday morning, she alluded to the report that L'Angelier had been poisoned, and she remarked that she had been in the habit of buying arsenic, as she had learned at school that it was good for the complexion. I had [already heard the] rumor that he had been poisoned. She said nothing further, and that was the last time I saw her.

"Before she made these statements to me, I was not aware that she was acquainted with L'Angelier. I was not acquainted with him myself."

Minnoch was excused and left the witness stand under Madeleine's watchful eye. His testimony had added nothing other than an exciting spectacle for the courtroom audience.

The *London Times* eagerly reported on even the slightest change in Madeleine's behavior: " . . . but in the course of the day [she] became a little more restless and excited than she had previously, and particularly when her former school companion, Miss Buchanan, and the gentleman to whom she was latterly engaged, Mr. Minnoch, were in the box."

Moncreiff addressed the topic of Madeleine's arsenic purchases by calling to the stand both of the apothecaries who had sold her the substance. The first was George Murdoch, from whom Madeleine made her initial purchase on February 21. He went over the details of the transaction, ending his testimony with: "I saw her again some three days after; she called and inquired if arsenic should not be white. I said it required to be sold mixed with something else. She did not purchase any more on that occasion."

George Carruthers Haliburton, an assistant in Currie's drug shop, testified about Madeleine's arsenic purchases on March 6 and 18.

"[I had never met Mary Jane Buchanan, who] accompanied Miss Smith on the first occasion. They were speaking together at the counter while I was putting up the arsenic. The young lady with Miss Smith remarked that she thought arsenic was white, and I said we had to color it according to the Act of Parliament.

"On the 18th, Mr. Currie made some objections—he said that we never sold it except to parties we knew and to parties of respectability, and he was about to refuse it when I told him that she had got it [from me] on a former occasion, and then we gave it to her. It was from the same bottle. A young lady, who, I suppose, was her sister, was with her. I had never seen the young lady who accompanied her on the second occasion before. She was a grown-up young lady—not the lady who was with her on the former occasion [of March 6].

"I never heard of arsenic, such as I gave Miss Smith, being used as a cosmetic."

Haliburton's testimony presents a puzzle: the "grown-up young lady" who accompanied Madeleine during her March 18 purchase. Mary Jane Buchanan was with her on March 6, but Madeleine's companion on the 18th is unknown. It might have been her sister, Bessie, or another of Madeleine's friends, but Madeleine makes no mention in her Declaration of being with anyone during that purchase. Even curiouser, neither legal team followed up on this loose end. Unless Haliburton was mistaken about Madeleine being in the company of another woman on March 18, this unknown lady is one more member of the very small group of people who knew Madeleine was buying arsenic.

A more trivial puzzle is whether Mr. Currie, in initially refusing the purchase of the 18th, was questioning Madeleine's frequency to his shop or her respectability.

Previous to the trial, the defense had made known their opinion that the letters and other documents had received careless handling after being secured as evidence. Wanting to formally address this topic before the defense had a chance to, Moncreiff presented several witnesses to testify about the documents' collection and storage. The first were Sheriff Officer John Murray and his assistant, Bernard MacLauchlin, who testified about their searches of Emile's office and lodgings and described the various papers and evidence they found in each location. Murray also stated that during the previous weeks he had unsuccessfully looked for Emile's signature in the Poison Books of apothecaries and drug shops in Glasgow, Stirling, Bridge of Allan, and along the road between Coatbridge and Glasgow.

The Glasgow joint Procurator-Fiscal testified regarding the condition of the letters themselves: "They were extremely difficult to decipher, and that made the transcribing of them a very slow and difficult process. They were in such a state originally, that they could not have been used to any extent by counsel in the case. Five persons in our own office copied the letters, and I think five clerks in the Sheriff-Clerk's office. They were not allowed to take them home, but I [later] learned that one or two of them had taken them home in the evening to copy."

Peter Taylor Young, one of the Procurator-Fiscal's staff, elaborated: "There were about 300 envelopes and 500 letters. They were extremely difficult to decipher, and I took fully ten days to read them all. I made a selection of them, with the view of reporting the case to the Crown. The utmost care was taken to restore the letters to their own envelopes. The investigation was a very serious interruption to the ordinary business of our office."

On July 3, Moncreiff suggested officially admitting all of Madeleine's letters as evidence. The defense objected, claiming that it would be unfair and unsafe to admit the letters, because their careless retrieval and storage could have resulted in tampering. Not only had the bulk of the letters been collected by William Stevenson, who was not a legal official (and who had testified that others from Huggins had looked through the letters), but some of the letters had been taken home overnight by various clerks for copying. Furthermore, the documents had not been housed by the Sheriff-Clerk, as was the norm, but by the Procurator-Fiscal. The prosecution argued that in this case the Procurator-Fiscal had held the documents under the direct orders of Lord Advocate Moncreiff.

The judges ruled that the defense's objection was not well-founded and declared that the letters would be read aloud the following day.

The controversy surrounding Madeleine's letters extended beyond the courtroom. On the same day that Moncreiff requested reading the letters aloud, John Inglis brought to the court's attention a claim by James Cunningham, editor of the *Scotch Thistle*. This newspaper stated that its next issue would feature *all* the letters Madeleine had written to Emile during their courtship. Although the entire correspondence had been copied for the private use of the court and the lawyers, only a few letters had been heretofore presented as evidence. Inglis questioned how this newspaper had obtained the remaining correspondence and maintained that the letters were confidential in nature and not for public viewing. Moncreiff, speaking for the prosecution team, said that he did not know of any way in which these letters could have fallen into the hands of anyone outside of the judges and the lawyers. The judges sent out a summons for James Cunningham, who heatedly denied that his newspaper would feature letters other than those few that had appeared as evidence. The Lord Justice-Clerk admonished him, saying that the statement in his newspaper was very "incautiously worded," and the gentleman was dismissed.

The recitation of Madeleine's letters took the entire day of July 4. Beginning with the first letter from March of 1855, they were read in a flat monotone by the elderly Clerk of the Court. Some accounts state that Madeleine showed no emotion throughout this process, while others reported that she occasionally buried her face in her hands. Some letters (or portions of letters) were considered too obscene and were excluded by the three judges, although a reporter for the *Durham Advertiser* would write: " . . . I have seen [complete] copies of these epistles . . . and I pray God I may never see such again. Ugh!"

The *London Times* reported: ". . . the prisoner scarcely maintained her jaunty, indifferent air during today's proceedings, but appeared to feel the exposure which her letters made."

After the letters had been read, Moncreiff proposed the reading aloud of the entries in Emile's diary notebook. Moncreiff argued that because the handwriting in the notebook had been confirmed by previous witnesses to be Emile's, the diary should be viewed as direct statements by Emile regarding his actions on each of the recorded dates. The defense countered, stating that the entries noted in the book could not be proven to have actually taken place, and some notations had already been contradicted by the prosecution's own witnesses. Furthermore, if Emile had not faithfully recorded the events as they happened, Inglis argued, he could have misremembered details in the period between an event and his notation of it. The judges decided to consider the matter and give their formal decision the next day of session.

The proceedings were then adjourned for thirty-six hours, as Court was not in session on Sundays. Madeleine passed the time of that Sunday, July 5, with the same small entertainments she had enjoyed during her long incarceration in Glasgow.

The judgment about the admissibility of Emile's diary notebook was the first order of business on Monday morning, July 6. All three judges admitted that it had been one of the most difficult legal questions they had ever encountered.

The Lord Justice-Clerk felt it odd that Emile started the diary only after he had received the abrupt letter from Madeleine asking for the return of her correspondence. He suspected Emile began this notebook to strengthen his influence over her, as he would then have not only her letters, but also notations regarding their meetings. As several of the diary's entries were "so short as to leave their meaning unexplained or doubtful," and since it was now impossible to question Emile regarding his motive behind keeping the notebook—or about the entries themselves—he could not legally admit it.

Lord Handyside agreed, stating that he found it curious that a person would begin a diary at any time other than the start of a calendar year. And he questioned whether the entries were made daily or if Emile wrote down an entire week's entries at one time—which would make the writing rely more on possibly faulty memory. Also, Handyside noted, because the writing was in pencil and the notebook had been transported to several locations before being secured as evidence, the writings could easily have been altered.

If Emile was living, Handyside went on, the notebook itself could not be legally presented as evidence, but could only be used by Emile in the witness box to refresh his memory. The notebook, he asserted, could not take a legal oath as to its truthfulness, nor could it be questioned or cross-examined. "It may be an idle, purposeless piece of writing. Or it may be a record of unfounded suspicions and malicious charges, treasured up by hostile and malignant feelings in a moody, spiteful mind."

Lord Ivory disagreed with the other two judges, saying that after reviewing other trials into which evidence similar to the notebook had been admitted, he was "totally unable to come to a conclusion that the evidence of this document should be excluded from the jury."

The majority of the three opinions formed the formal ruling, and the notebook and its entries were kept from the jury, who were then brought into the courtroom.

The diary issue settled, Moncreiff called his final witness, Mrs. Janet Anderson. This was the woman who, according to Madeleine's letters, had been extremely active in spreading gossip about Madeleine's new necklace and her engagement to Minnoch: "I am acquainted with the prisoner. I recollect meeting her at a party in my house on the 5th of February. I met her also at a party at Mrs. Wilkie's shortly before she was at my house. She had a necklace on. I asked her from whom she had got it. She said she had got it from Papa. I asked if she had got it from Mr. Minnoch, and she denied that. I don't recollect if I spoke of this to anybody. I may have mentioned that I thought she got it from Mr. Minnoch."

Mrs. Anderson was excused, and Moncreiff declared that the case, on behalf of the Crown, was completed.

After a brief recess, John Inglis began his case for the defense by stating that some of his first witnesses would be discussing Emile's earlier life, and Inglis was unwilling to name, or to have a witness name, any persons who did not need to be so identified. He then requested that the prosecution, in their cross-examination of the defense's witnesses, adhere to this principle. The prosecution agreed, and so the exact identity of the "Lady from Fife," who had rejected Emile, would never be known.

In contrast to the lengthy questioning of the prosecution's witnesses, Inglis moved his thirty-one witnesses on and off the stand at a rapid pace, beginning and ending his presentation on July 6th.

The first defense witness was Robert Baker, a grocer from Jersey who had lodged with Emile in 1851 at Edinburgh's Rainbow Tavern, which Baker's uncle owned. Baker painted a picture of Emile as a despondent and suicidal man: "He was very easily excited and, at times, subject to low spirits. [Once], before he went to Dundee, he told me he was tired of his existence and wished himself out of the world—he said [so] on more than one occasion. I remember on one occasion he got out of bed and went to the window. I rose out of bed and went to him, and he said that if I had not disturbed him, he would have thrown himself out. He was not crying—he was very cool and collected, and did not seem at all exited or agitated. [Another time,] we walked to Leith Pier. When there, he said he had a great mind to throw himself over one morning, because he was quite tired of his existence. I have seen him reading newspaper accounts of suicide, and I have heard him say that here was a person who had the courage that he should have had, that he wished he had the same courage, or something to that effect. I [once] received [a] letter from L'Angelier [saying]: 'I never was so unhappy in my life. I wish I had the courage to blow my brains out.'

"I happened to know that he had at that time met with a disappointment in a love matter. He did not tell me so himself, but I heard my uncle talk of it. I heard L'Angelier speak to other people about it. It was about some lady in Fife. He was in distress about not having a situation, in order to enable him to keep his engagement with her."

Next called was William Pringle Laird, the nurseryman from Dundee who had hired Emile to work at his seed shop in 1852. He would be the first of several witnesses to recount Emile's brief residence in Dundee. He stated that the dead man had been a good worker, although "excitable and changeable in his temper: sometimes very melancholy and sometimes very blithesome.

"It was a fortnight or a month after he came that he said he had been crossed in love. He told me it was reported the girl was to be married to another, but that he could scarcely believe it, because he did not think she could take another. I understood that that was because she was pledged to him. I believe she was in the middle station of life. After this I saw her marriage in the newspapers. L'Angelier did see that notice. I said what I could to soothe him. He said he was very miserable, and that he wished he was out of the world, or words to that effect."

William Pringle, an apprentice to Laird in 1852, took the stand next and outlined Emile's reaction to learning of his former beloved's marriage: "He ran once or twice behind the counter, then he took hold of the counter knife. He did not point it at himself, but he held it out. When I stepped forward, he put it down again. I don't remember what he said. I don't think he was shedding tears. I did not observe him crying. He was particularly melancholy for some time after this occurrence."

William Anderson, another Dundee nurseryman who had known Emile, testified next regarding Emile's general interactions with women: "He boasted of his success with ladies. I remember on one occasion, particularly in my own house at supper, he told me he was very intimate with two ladies in Dundee at the time, and that it seemed to him his attachment for them was returned—that they were very beautiful girls and worth a considerable sum of money."

The Lord Justice-Clerk asked the witness if Emile meant that he had been successful in seducing them: "No, it was that he loved them and they loved him in return. I did not put this down as a piece of bragging. I thought it was in earnest. He said he did not know very well what he would do if he was jilted, and he said something to the effect he would revenge on them in some shape or other."

William MacDougal Ogilvie, a member of the Horticultural Society that met regularly at Laird's shop, testified that Emile spoke of working in France for a person of very high station, who entrusted Emile with all travel arrangements: "He said [when] the horses were very much knocked up that he had given them arsenic. He said he gave it to them to make them accomplish the journey. I asked what effect this had. He said it made them long-winded, and thus made them able to accomplish a feat. I said, was he not afraid of poisoning them? He said no—so far from doing that, he had taken it himself. I told him I should not like to try it, and he seemed to say he had not felt any bad effects from it, that there had been no danger, or expressions to that effect. He mentioned another effect of arsenic, which was that it improved the complexion. I inferred from his remarks that he took it for that purpose. He also said that he complained of pains in his back, and had a little difficulty in breathing, and he said it had a good effect in that way.

"I have seen him on more than one occasion eat poppy seeds in large quantities—in handfuls—in the shop. I expressed surprise, and he said that, so far from being dangerous, it was much better than filberts and that he took it in large quantities. He said he had taken the poppy seeds in such quantities that he had got quite giddy with them. He said he had done that when he was in Dicksons and Company."

Ogilvie's testimony would be reinforced by the next witness, David Hill of Dundee, who testified that Emile had told him that he took arsenic "regularly."

The next witness, Edward Vokes Mackay, a Dublin merchant who occasionally visited Edinburgh, did not paint a flattering portrait of Emile: "I had several conversations with him. I saw quite enough of him to enable me to form an opinion of his character and disposition. I formed anything but a good opinion of him. I considered him a vain, lying fellow. He was very boastful of his personal appearance and parties admiring him, ladies particularly. He boasted of his acquaintances repeatedly, and the high society he had moved in. He mentioned several titled people whom he had met, but not believing anything he was saying at the time, I did not store up any of their titles.

"He said ladies admired him often. I remember, on one occasion particularly, he came in when I was reading the papers in the Rainbow [Tavern], and he told me he met a lady in Princes Street with another lady, and she had remarked what pretty feet he had. I had once said he was a rather pretty little person, and he had gone out and concocted the story that she had said she admired his feet. I never believed anything he said afterwards.

"Shortly before he went to Dundee, I met him one evening in Princes Street Gardens. I could not say the date, but he went to Dundee the following day. He was sitting in the Garden—I came on him accidentally—he had his head in his cambric pocket handkerchief, and I put my hand on him and said his name. He held up his head, and I perceived he had been crying. He mentioned that a lady in Fifeshire had slighted him, but I made light of the matter. He made a long complaint about her family—he was much excited.

"To a certain extent, I believed the story about the Fife lady. I believed there was a lady there and that he was after her, for I had seen him weep about it."

Janet B. Christie, the next witness on the stand, knew Emile through a mutual acquaintance. She had heard him say on one occasion that French women used arsenic for their complexion. Overall, Christie thought him "a rather forward man and full of pretension."

Switching from the topic of Emile's past to that of Madeleine's, Inglis called Agnes MacMillan to the stand. MacMillan had been a maid for the Smith family before Madeleine and Emile had met, and she testified: "On one occasion [Madeleine] spoke to me about arsenic. I can't remember what brought on the conversation, but I perfectly remember her saying that she believed arsenic was used for the complexion, or that it was good for the complexion—I don't recollect which."

Inglis then brought to the stand a succession of three men—a surgeon, a druggist, and a shopkeeper—who had been approached by customers wanting arsenic for cosmetic purposes after reading about such practices in popular magazines. All three men had refused the requests.

The Lord Justice-Clerk interrupted this stream of witnesses to warn Inglis that this type of evidence was "very loose," since rumors about the case had been circulating for some time, and people might invent stories involving arsenic for the sole purpose of being called as a witness in a popular trial.

Returning then to the topic of Emile's past, Inglis called to the stand William D'Esterre Roberts, a friend of the dead man. Dining with Roberts on Christmas Day of 1853, Emile had became violently ill after eating and had to be taken home.

"I knew L'Angelier pretty well. I always thought him a nice little fellow. He sat in the church three years—at that time I would not have hesitated to believe his word. I had occasion [later] to change my opinion of him."

When asked why his opinion had changed, Roberts admitted that it was due to the gossip after Emile's death, and not from his own personal experiences with the man. Inglis quickly dismissed Roberts from the stand, calling next the two Baird brothers, from whom Emile had sought an introduction to Madeleine in 1855.

The elder brother, Charles, testified that Emile had implored him to perform an introduction to Madeleine, and also recalled a time during the autumn of 1856 when Emile was very ill. His younger brother, Robert, then testified about the actual introduction that took place outside Paterson's Draper's Shop on Sauchiehall Street in 1855: "I recollect him asking me to introduce him to Miss Smith. I cannot say how long ago that is—I think it is about two years ago. He asked me several times to introduce him, and he seemed very pressing about it. I introduced them on the street. Mr. L'Angelier did not ask me to introduce him to Miss Smith's father, but he expressed an anxiety or determination to be introduced to him.

"L'Angelier asked me to go with him once to Row, and I understood his purpose was to go and see Miss Smith. He might have said he wished to call at Rowaleyn, but I don't recollect."

One obvious risk of *running her letters*, and hurrying a case to trial, was the lack of time for a legal team to speak to their witnesses before they were actually called to the stand.

The testimony of the next witness, Lieutenant Colonel Robert Fraser, provided a light moment in an otherwise intensive day of questioning: "I reside at Portobello. I was not acquainted with the late Mr. L'Angelier. I never saw him in my life, to my knowledge. He never was in my house, and never dined with me. At the time of his death, I received a note from Mr. George McCall mentioning the fact of his death. He mentioned him as a mutual friend. But I was very much surprised at it, never having [met] Mr. L'Angelier or Mr. McCall. There is no other Colonel Fraser in Portobello, but there is a Captain Fraser, R.N."

Inglis then moved on to a critical phase of his presentation. Over the course of the next several witnesses, Inglis attempted to prove that the healthy man who had accompanied the auctioneer, Thomas Ross, on his walk from Coatbridge to Glasgow on March 22 was not Emile.

The first of these witnesses was Dr. Charles Adam from Coatbridge. The Coatbridge train station is the closest to Glasgow for a traveler coming from the north, the direction of Bridge of Allan: "On Sunday afternoon, March 22, I was in my druggist's shop. I remember a man coming into the shop that afternoon. He asked, at first, for twenty-five drops of laudanum, which I gave him. After he got the laudanum, he asked for a bottle of soda water. I said we had no soda water, but I would give him a soda powder, which I did. He took it. I took him to be a military man—there were several about Drumpeller at the time. He wore a mustache."

Dr. Adam was then shown Emile's portrait: "This has a resemblance to the person, but I could not be quite certain it is the same—it is like the gentleman. My shop was dark at the time, so I could scarcely observe, because we don't take off the shutters on Sunday. We get the light in by the glass door. I suppose that he had on a dark brownish coat and a Balmoral bonnet."

Dr. James Dickson, another druggist along the road between Glasgow and Coatbridge, said a man came into his shop on a Sunday, "sometime in the end of March." The man was also given laudanum. Dickson stated that the portrait of Emile is "extremely like the person who called at my shop."

Miss Jane Kirk, an assistant in her brother's druggist shop in Glasgow, remembered a man coming into the shop on a Sunday. "I think it was in March, but I can't say what day of the month. I think it was about the end of the month. It was a little before or after eight o'clock."

The man bought some medicine ("a powder") from Kirk and took it away with him, although she did not recall the exact medicine. When shown the portrait of Emile, she said: "It is as like him as anything I have ever seen. It is as good a likeness as I have ever seen. I was struck by his appearance at the time, and I noticed it particularly. He paid for the medicine. He took the money from a little purse." She was then shown Emile's purse, a common one of the day. "This is the purse."

Representatives from *Chambers' Journal* and *Blackwood's Magazine* took the stand next and verified that those periodicals had previously featured articles concerning the various uses of arsenic.

Inglis then reread two of Madeleine's letters where she was reacting to apparent suicide threats on Emile's part, illustrating that Emile's tendency toward self-destructive behavior continued well into his relationship with Madeleine.

Dr. Robert Paterson, a physician in Leith and the next witness, stated that he had treated cases of attempted suicide by arsenic ingestion, mostly by female mill workers. Paterson said of deaths due to arsenic poisoning: "sickness and vomiting ceased in most cases an hour or two before death, but in some instances continued till death. Death resulted in thirty-six hours, and [once] in twelve hours, from the commencement of the symptoms."

Shifting topics again, Inglis attempted to prove how Emile could have pilfered a small amount of arsenic without having to sign a Poison Book. Inglis called to the stand a storekeeper and a manufacturing chemist, both of whom kept quantities of arsenic at their Glasgow businesses. Each man testified that while the arsenic was locked up at night, it was uncovered, unguarded, and completely accessible during the day.

Janet Smith, Madeleine's thirteen-year-old sister, was the next witness—the only one of the Smith family who appeared in court, either as a witness or merely to show support.

"I remember Sunday, March 22. We went to bed at the same time that night—I am quite sure of that. We went to bed about half past ten or after that. We went downstairs together from the dining room. I don't remember which was in bed first. We were both undressing at the same time, and we both got into bed nearly about the same time. We usually take about a half hour to undress. We were in no particular hurry that night in undressing. My sister was in bed with me before I was asleep—I am quite sure of that. She was undressed as usual, and in her nightclothes. I don't know which of us fell asleep first. It was not long after we went to bed before I fell asleep. On the Monday morning, March 23, I found my sister in bed when I awoke about eight."

On the topic of Madeleine's flight to Row, Janet stated: "I remember the morning that Madeleine went away. I suppose she had been in bed that night. I was asleep before she came to bed. She was away when I woke.

"I don't remember Papa making a present of a necklace to my sister lately. I remember him doing so about a year ago.

"I have seen my sister take cocoa. I never saw her make it in her room. She kept it in a paper in her room. I have seen my sister taking cocoa in the dining room. I don't know that she had been recommended to take it. No other body in the house took it. She took it in the dining room, but kept it in her own room."

Dr. James Adam Lawrie, a Glasgow physician, testified that he had tried a mixture of arsenic and water on his face and hands, as Madeleine claimed to have done, and found "it had a softening effect. . . . I would have no hesitation in repeating the experiment."

Dr. Douglas MacIagan, a physician in Edinburgh, reinforced Dr. Lawrie's testimony, saying that washing in arsenic and water would be harmless, as most of the poison would sink to the bottom and not come into direct contact with the skin.

After a final witness who confirmed the various distances between Alloa, Bridge of Allan, Stirling, Coatbridge, and the Great Western Road in Glasgow, John Inglis rested the defense's case, and the court adjourned just prior to five o'clock in the evening.

The trial and its witness testimony continued to be the leading topic of conversation in shops and houses. The *Ayrshire Express* reported: "Eager crowds gather in the early morning at the gaol, and in Parliament-Square, to catch a glimpse of the prisoner as she is taken to the court. In the evening thousands gather in the streets to see the cab in which she is borne back from the courtroom to the prison. . . . Hundreds are passed in for a few minutes by official friends to get a glimpse at the prisoner, and may be seen departing with the air of satisfied curiosity upon their anxious countenances.

"The newspapers, in the second, third, and forth editions with which the town is deluged, stop the presses to tell how she looked at a particular hour . . . and how for breakfast she had coffee, rolls, and a mutton chop, which she ate with great apparent heartiness."

On Tuesday, July 7, Moncreiff began the prosecution's address to the jury by stating that it was his "painful public duty" to present this case. There was, Moncreiff assured the jury, no "possibility of escape for the unhappy prisoner from the net that she has woven for herself." He then outlined the indictments: two counts of administering poison with intent to kill, and one count of successful and fatal administration of poison.

Moncreiff then stated what he stressed was a plain fact: Emile died of ingestion of arsenic. All postmortem examinations found arsenic in every organ examined.

To remove the possible stigma of someone tampering with Madeleine's correspondence, Moncreiff outlined the letters' trail, starting with their discovery by Stevenson and Kennedy, and stated that they had always been carefully handled.

Moncreiff then quickly related the history of Madeleine and Emile's relationship. He refused to comment on Emile's character, because the facts presented "make it impossible to speak of him in any terms but those of very strong condemnation." Although, he strongly reminded the jury, three of his landladies and many of his friends and coworkers spoke favorably of him during their testimony and, by energy and attention, Emile had worked his way up to a "respectable" position.

The relationship between Madeleine and Emile progressed, according to Moncreiff, and took on a "criminal aspect" when their sexual union was consummated, which was then followed by repeated acts of "improper connection."

When Madeleine "cooled" and Emile threatened to take her letters to her father, she "saw the position she was in" and feared great shame and the end of her engagement to William Minnoch. She pleaded for the return of the letters, but he refused. And then: "There is one interview—she attempts to buy prussic acid. There is another interview—she bought arsenic. There is a third interview—she bought arsenic again."

Do not be swayed by the lack of eyewitnesses, Moncreiff warned, because the very nature of poisoning makes it secretive, and "if it was done with a guilty conscience, it was done secretly." The jury's obligation is to "trace the crime from the course of the circumstances."

Moncreiff then went through the general themes of her letters, saying the ones after their sexual union "are written in a strain that I do not think I should comment upon." And if the defense claimed that Emile corrupted "her moral sense" he would not deny that—but it is irrelevant. He pointed out letters where she speaks of Emile "loving" her, and emphasized that there were "three [under]scores being made under [the word] 'love'!" It cannot be misinterpreted what was going on between the two, and she was not an unwilling victim.

Moncreiff thereupon illustrated, through the letters, the growing presence of Minnoch and explained how the letters had been chronologically arranged by postmarks and evidence within the letters themselves. He then went on to show how easily a person inside the Blythswood Square house could move about at night without alerting others.

To bring Madeleine's honesty into question, Moncreiff read aloud various passages of her letters where she repeatedly "vows" herself to Emile, while, Moncreiff maintained, she was simultaneously being courted by Minnoch. Focusing on the February 2 letter, where Madeleine harshly broke off her relationship with Emile, Moncreiff reminded the jury that only four days previously she had accepted Minnoch's marriage proposal. In that letter, she stated "coolness" as the sole reason for breaking her engagement with Emile—when, in fact, she was now engaged to another man. She wrote that letter "in the hope that his indignant spirit would induce him to turn her off, when she would be free to form another engagement. But, gentlemen, she had the dreadful recollection of the existence of the correspondence. She did not know how much L'Angelier had, but she knew that she was completely in his power."

When L'Angelier threatened to show Madeleine's letters to her father, it may have been dishonorable, but "I do not see how he, as a man of honor, could allow this marriage with Mr. Minnoch to take place and remain silent." Moncreiff admitted that while the two may not legally have been man and wife, their letters clearly showed that they both *believed* themselves to be so. And, as he believed Madeleine was his wife, Emile had the right to refuse to return her letters.

The two February 1857 letters in which Madeleine pleaded for mercy also included lies about her engagement to Minnoch, Moncreiff pointed out: "She is so committed that she cannot extricate herself, and yet, if not extricated, her character, her fame, her reputation, her position, are forfeited forever."

Moncreiff then addressed Madeleine's attempted prussic acid purchase. Has anyone in the jury, Moncreiff asked, ever heard of this substance being used as a cosmetic, her claimed intent? Obviously, Moncreiff maintained, Madeleine was starting to think of poisons and excuses for wanting them.

Madeleine's statement to Monsieur de Mean that Emile had never been inside the Blythswood Square house was a lie, Moncreiff declared, and had been directly contradicted by Christina Haggart's testimony.

Regarding the first two illnesses, Moncreiff stated that the prosecution had presented evidence showing that Madeleine and Emile did meet the night before Emile's first illness of February 19 (Moncreiff wisely chose not to address the discrepancy about the date of that first illness), and the evidence regarding the second illness of February 22 was even stronger. The prosecution, by presenting as evidence the letter where Madeleine had said, "you did look bad Sunday night and Monday morning," proved that the couple had met prior to Emile's second illness—as this letter was written, Moncreiff maintained, on Wednesday, February 25, four days after her first purchase of arsenic on the 21st. This letter is dated only by the word *Wednesday*, however, and Inglis would later dismiss this document as possibly referring to any Wednesday during Madeleine and Emile's relationship.

Moncreiff then addressed Madeleine's reasoning for purchasing arsenic: "She says she had been told when at school in England, by a Miss Guibilei, that arsenic is good for the complexion. She came from school in 1853, and, singularly enough, it is not till that week of February [of 1857] prior to the 22nd that she ever thinks of arsenic for that purpose. Why, gentlemen, should that be? At that moment I have shown you she was frightened at the danger she was in in the highest degree—and is it likely that at that time she was looking for a new cosmetic? [And] if she was following out what she found in the magazines, that was not what she found there: for they say that the way to use arsenic is internally." Moncreiff also questioned the results of Madeleine's first supposed cosmetic "wash" with arsenic: were the results so great that the treatment was worth repeating, which she claimed to have done?

Madeleine had suggested, after her first two alleged poisoning attempts, that Emile go to the Isle of Wight. ". . . Probably she thought that if she could get him out of the way she might have her marriage with Mr. Minnoch over without [Emile's] knowledge, after which it would be easy to get her letters, as there would be no motive for keeping them."

Emile's journey from Bridge of Allan to Glasgow, Moncreiff said, showed that Emile was healthy and fit, negating Inglis's story of the mysterious man who had repeatedly stopped for medicine. Similarly, Moncreiff discounted Constable Thomas Kavan's not seeing Emile in the Blythswood Square area on that final night—as he hadn't seen Emile on numerous other nights when the deceased had undoubtedly been in the area.

Addressing the possibility of Emile's committing suicide, Moncreiff pointed out that on his deathbed Emile said he wanted to recover; and if he truly thought he was dying, he would have sent for Madeleine, whom he loved, rather than for Miss Perry. Although, Moncreiff conceded, if he had lived long enough to see Miss Perry, "We should [know] more about this case than we do now."

Continuing on the topic of suicide, Moncreiff dismissed the testimony of witnesses who said that Emile had talked of killing himself, because at those times he was in "a poorer class in life," and those same witnesses also said he tended to boast and exaggerate. Additionally, in all of those situations, there was another person present to whom Emile told his suicidal intentions. A suicidal person does the act, Moncreiff stated, he does not announce it to others. Furthermore, Moncreiff asserted, Emile was cheerful at the prospect of seeing Madeleine that night, so why would he kill himself: "Is it in the least likely that a man in his position would go out to Blythswood Square and swallow dry arsenic there, and then totter home and die?" And where, Moncreiff asked, would Emile have obtained the poison at that time of night?

Speaking on Madeleine's behavior after Emile's death, Moncreiff continued: "apparently the prisoner had shown no particular agitation at the news of L'Angelier's death," and he reminded the jury that her subsequent flight to Rowaleyn had never been fully explained by her or by the defense.

Moncreiff neared the completion of his presentation by addressing several minor conjectural issues: arsenic was never used in the manner Madeleine stated by either Miss Guibilei or in any magazine articles; it was meaningless that nobody in the Blythswood Square home heard any noise on the night of March 22, as there had been other nights when Emile had visited Madeleine without anyone's knowledge; and if the prosecution's supposition was correct that Emile's first two illnesses were Madeleine's unskilled attempts to poison Emile, "there is nothing surprising in the fact that the third dose was a very large quantity."

Having thoroughly recounted his case and the evidence, Moncreiff concluded: "I see no outlet for this unhappy prisoner, and if you come to the same result as I have done, there is but one course open to you, and that is to return a verdict of guilty of this charge."

There was a brief silence as Moncreiff sat down. After some whispered conversation among the three judges, it was decided to delay John Inglis's address until the following day, and the court was adjourned at 3:30 P.M.

At the opening of the proceedings the following morning, July 8, John Inglis rose and addressed the jury: "Gentlemen of the jury, the charge against the prisoner is murder, and the punishment of murder is death—and that simple statement is sufficient to suggest to us the awful solemnity of the occasion which brings you and me face to face."

Inglis then began his concluding address for the defense, outlining Emile's melancholy life and his numerous failed romances prior to meeting Madeleine. Once he had seen her, Emile made desperate attempts to gain an introduction to Madeleine, and Inglis called Robert Baird's eventual introduction an "indiscretion" on Baird's part.

Regarding Madeleine and Emile's early association, Inglis pointed out that Madeleine's earliest letters were proper and dignified. It was Emile who tried to win her, seduce her, corrupt her—while she dutifully tried to stop the correspondence on four separate occasions. As to their sexual union: "How vile the arts which he resorted to for accomplishing his nefarious purpose. She had [not] lost her virtue merely, but . . . her sense of decency. This was his doing."

Inglis stated that communication at Blythswood Square was difficult for the two—more so than at India Street. In many of her Blythswood Square letters, Madeleine cautioned Emile not to make any noise at the window and alert her family to his presence. They had few opportunities to meet, as Janet slept with her every night and her parents were rarely away from home. Such meetings were totally dependent on the enlisted aid of Christina Haggart, and the maid had testified that she knew of only two such meetings in the Blythswood Square home.

Addressing each of the charges separately, Inglis told the jury that the first charge of attempted poisoning should be disregarded entirely. The date of Emile's first illness was in conflict between Mary Perry's and Ann Jenkins's testimonies—Perry placing it firmly on February 19, and Jenkins believing it to have occurred around the 13th of that month. Regardless of either version, both dates fell before Madeleine made her first purchase of arsenic on February 21. Inglis summed up: "Either he was ill from arsenic poisoning on the morning of the 20th [of February], or he was not. If he was, he had received arsenic from other hands than the prisoner's. If he was not, the foundation of the whole [prosecution's] case is shaken. So much for the first charge."

Regarding the second charge, Inglis reminded the jury that Madeleine's first purchase of arsenic occurred on February 21. But, Inglis pointed out, the prosecution never proved, in any form, that a meeting actually took place between Madeleine and Emile on the 21st or 22nd—nor was there mention in any of Madeleine's letters of such a rendezvous. And Mrs. Jenkins had testified, Inglis reminded the jury, that Emile had not asked for the pass key on the night of the 21st.

Inglis began addressing the murder charge by presenting a timeline of Madeleine and Emile's movements in the weeks leading up to his death. Madeleine and her family left for the Bridge of Allan on March 6 and did not return until the 17th. Emile had left for Edinburgh on March 10 and also returned on the 17th. Mrs. Jenkins clearly testified, Inglis reminded the jury, that Emile had stayed at home all day on the 18th and left for Bridge of Allan early on the morning of the 19th. He returned the night of his death and asked Mrs. Jenkins for the pass key. Given the fact that Emile did not experience an occurrence of the stomach illness in early March (the only time at which both Madeleine and Emile were in Glasgow), Inglis's timeline implied that there was no time in which Madeleine had met Emile, let alone tried to poison him, during the entire period of time between her first arsenic purchase on February 21 and his death more than one month later.

Speaking on the final week of Emile's life, Inglis reminded the jury that Madeleine wrote Emile the "lost" letter, which proposed a meeting. But, as Emile's letter to Mary Perry stated, it arrived too late after being forwarded to him in Edinburgh for him to actually meet with her, insinuating that Emile was fully conscious of the one-day delay his letters from Madeleine were experiencing. (As an aside, Inglis blamed the prosecution and the Crown authorities for losing this vital letter, because both Madeleine's and Thuau's accompanying envelopes had survived.) Madeleine wrote her final letter on Friday the 20th, completely unaware that Emile was away from Glasgow. Inglis asserted that the final meeting was planned for Saturday night, the 21st—and not Sunday the 22nd. And, considering their history and the complex planning it took for them to meet, and because Emile knew that her letters were taking an extra day to arrive, Inglis firmly maintained that Emile would not have come to see her unexpectedly on Sunday, and Madeleine would not have received him even if he had.

Next, Inglis questioned Emile's journey from Bridge of Allan to Glasgow on Sunday, March 22. Inglis pointed out that the auctioneer, Thomas Ross, the prosecution's witness who had supposedly accompanied Emile on the long walk to Glasgow, was not shown Emile's portrait for identification, as most other prosecution witnesses were—which was odd and "a very remarkable omission on the part of the Crown." Nor were any of the people from the inn at Coatbridge, where Emile allegedly ate, called forth as witnesses and asked to identify him by that portrait. Mr. Ross had also testified that the man with whom he walked had come from Alloa and had even known the correct walking distance to Stirling from Alloa—but had never mentioned Bridge of Allan. The man accompanying Ross also said that he had tried to cash a check in Stirling but had been refused, although the prosecution had neither proved that Emile had attempted this nor found the refused check among his possessions. Unmistakably, Inglis maintained, Emile was the ill man who stopped three times for medicine on the way to Glasgow. At the final store, Inglis reminded the jury, Emile purchased from Jane Kirk, but did not consume, some kind of powder.

According to the prosecution's case, Inglis stated, Emile himself was suspicious of being poisoned when he dined with Mary Perry's sister and brother-in-law on March 16. Nothing occurred between March 16 and March 22 that would have changed his mind on this concern, but the Crown now expected the jury to believe he willingly ingested it again "with all his previous suspicion that [Madeleine] was practicing on his life." This is even more unbelievable, Inglis asserted, compounded by the fact that he took from her a larger dose than had ever reportedly been used before.

Dr. Penny's experiments with Currie's and Murdoch's arsenic clearly showed the supplementary coloring matter in the dogs' digestive tracts. Presence of such coloring matter in Emile's body, Inglis stated, would have been a concrete way to connect Madeleine's arsenic to Emile—but the Crown did not direct any of the postmortem doctors to look for it. Why was that? Inglis asked.

Inglis emphasized that Madeleine had made her purchases of arsenic very openly, even having a companion with her on one occasion. Additionally, Madeleine purchased arsenic the morning of the day she accompanied her family on an extended trip to Bridge of Allan. If her intent was to poison Emile, Inglis asked, why would she buy it at that time? She bought the arsenic and then immediately went *away* from him. She did not expect him to be at Bridge of Allan, as she had specifically told him not to go there.

She had used the arsenic incorrectly as a cosmetic, Inglis explained, because she had misremembered the magazine article that reported how mountain climbers used it for their complexion. And several druggists had testified, Inglis reminded the jury, that other women had come to them desiring arsenic for cosmetic purposes.

Inglis then summed up Emile's character: a boaster who talked of suicide "but whether he met his death by suicide, or whether he met his death by accident, or however he met his death, the question for you is—is this murder proved?"

When Madeleine asked for her letters back and Emile refused, "he must have been dead to all feelings of humanity, or he would never have refrained from burning those letters. But he not only preserves them, he retains them as an engine of power and oppression in his hands." His reason? To possess her and marry her to raise his social status.

Inglis emphasized that three things must be unconditionally proven in order to find Madeleine guilty of this crime: possession of poison; death by that poison; and, most importantly, the opportunity to administer that poison.

Inglis then moved on to the question of motive. Inglis asserted that motive must mean more than the fact that Emile's death would have been advantageous for Madeleine—for who does not have that same motive for murder: an eldest son has the same motive to kill his father, and a young soldier has the same motive to kill all his senior officers. And, Inglis questioned, what advantage would Madeleine really have if Emile died? She knew fully well that her correspondence would still exist. Inglis maintained that her greatest desire was to avoid shame, but Emile's death would naturally "lead to the immediate exposure of everything."

She fled to Row, Inglis stated, because she feared the letters coming out and her secrets being revealed. If she were fleeing from a murder she had committed, Inglis maintained, she would have picked a faster method of transport than a steamship, as her two pursuers easily caught up with her. On her return, "the moment she was met by a charge of being implicated in causing the death of L'Angelier, she at once assumed the courage of a heroine."

Her Declaration was true and no part of it had been disproved by the Crown, Inglis insisted. Addressing one possible discrepancy, Inglis explained that Madeleine knew of Emile's trip to Bridge of Allan at the time of her Declaration because she had been told of it by Monsieur de Mean after Emile's death—but she did not know of the trip at the time of Emile's actual journey.

As for Madeleine's almost unnatural calmness throughout all the legal proceedings, Inglis compared her to Eliza Fenning, a London servant who had been accused of poisoning her employers. Eliza showed similar calmness throughout her trial—and at her execution. Much later, a man on his deathbed confessed to those killings. Madeleine showed no signs of guilt, Inglis maintained, because she had none.

Inglis then brought his summation to a close with the fiery conclusion: "May the spirit of all truth guide you to an honest, a just, and a true verdict!"

The Lord Justice-Clerk then formally addressed the jury, telling them that their verdict should rest on the evidence alone, although he conceded that poisoning often relies on circumstantial evidence. Court was then adjourned for the day.

The court session for July 9 officially began with the Lord Justice-Clerk giving his charge to the jury. He discussed the evidence presented by both sides and told the jury to weigh those two sides against each other, but conceded that the evidence surrounding Emile's first illness, the content of the first charge against Madeleine, was very weak. He further acknowledged that the handling of the letters was "loose, irregular, and slovenly," but that "it did not appear that the panel [the legal term for the defendant] had suffered any prejudice from the want of any of them."

Speaking of the events initiated by Madeleine's final letter, the Lord Justice-Clerk suggested that she could easily have waited for him a second night if he did not appear the first night. Inglis hurriedly interjected that she did not wait the second night—she waited only Saturday night and this fact was the turning point of the case and must be completely clear. The Lord Justice-Clerk then stated the three charges:

1. Madeleine administered poison to Emile on the 19th or 20th of February.

2. Madeleine administered poison to Emile on the 22nd of February.

3. Madeleine administered poison to Emile on the night of March 22, which directly led to his death.

In regard to the actual charges, the Lord Justice-Clerk said, "I think it my duty to tell you, as a judge, that on that [first] charge you should find her not guilty. But we are in a very different situation as to the illness of the 22nd [of February] and the morning of the 23rd [of March]."

Amid much whispering by the audience and reporters, the men of the jury withdrew at approximately 1:10 in the afternoon.

As she had done each previous day of the trial, Madeleine declined any lunch or beverage at midday. The spectators talked among themselves, some straining to get a quick look at Madeleine as she sat facing the front of the courtroom.

In Scotland's jury system of the time, a majority vote among the jurors, and not a unanimous decision, determined the verdict. There were three possible verdicts: *guilty*, which would lead to a death sentence, *not guilty*, and *not proven*.

At 1:32 P.M., less than thirty minutes after retiring, the jury returned and the Lord Justice-Clerk called for silence. In the tense stillness, the verdicts were announced: the jury found Madeleine *not guilty* on the first charge, and *not proven* on the second and third charges. The vote had been thirteen to two on all three verdicts, with the two dissenters finding her *guilty* on all three counts.

The courtroom audience exploded into wild cheers, and the noisy chaos quickly spread to the anxious crowds outside the courthouse.

Madeleine reportedly smiled only after the third verdict had been read, and John Inglis rested his head in his hands, but said nothing to his client.

The three judges attempted to silence the crowd, but the shouting and stamping of feet only increased. Aggravated, the Lord Justice-Clerk singled out one of the courtroom spectators and had the man brought before him. After staring at him in stony silence, he said: "This court has ordered you to its bar as an offender against its rules—but after looking at you, we do not think you are worthy to stand even in that position. You appear a very stupid person. Foolish, silly, fellow! Go away!"

The courtroom crowd poured out onto the steps of the courthouse to witness Madeleine's triumphant exit and return to freedom. They were not disappointed: a carriage drove up and a veiled lady and two police officers bolted from the courthouse doors and into the vehicle. The coach then sped off in the direction of the prison, the noisy throng following closely behind.

The *London Times* reported on the impact of the verdict: "With regard to the prisoner, she had awaited the issue with great calmness and composure, although there were occasional evidences in her veiled countenance how great her effort was so to sustain herself. When the verdict was concluded, she seemed more moved than she had been throughout the trial. One of her agents, an elderly gentleman, who had occasionally spoken to her a cheery word throughout the morning, as well as on previous days, shook her warmly by the hand, as did also the female warder who had sat beside her throughout the trial.

"The excitement which has been shown out of doors since the trial commenced was at its height on Thursday afternoon, when the trial concluded. Several thousand persons awaited the result outside the court, and on learning it repeated the cheers which had been so loudly vented within the court. The newspaper offices were immediately besieged by eager crowds, and many thousand copies were sold by different journals before evening set in. Great anxiety was shown to get a sight of the prisoner, but she did not leave the court till nearly three o'clock, and did so comparatively unobserved; [and then] drove, we believe, to a roadside railway station, but her place of asylum was very properly not made known."

It was later revealed that the veiled female who had sprinted into the carriage was not Madeleine, but a young lady from the courtroom's audience. John Wilkie, Madeleine's initial defense lawyer, convinced the woman to exchange clothes with Madeleine and make the hasty exit in order to distract the crowds. The young lady, who had attended most (if not all) of the days of the trial, would receive for her efforts the honor of actually meeting Madeleine as they hurriedly exchanged clothes. After the crowd had entirely dispersed, Madeleine quietly left the courthouse on foot, accompanied only by her brother, Jack. Getting into a cab in the High Street, they traveled to Slateford, and then caught a train to Greenock. They arrived at Rowaleyn at ten o'clock that night—Madeleine walking into an undoubtedly chilly family reception.

The jury's decision in no way curbed the debate about the case, and possible solutions, both plausible and bizarre, would continue to be presented and discussed in the years following the trial. However, barring the existence of any significant facts about the case that have never come to light, there are only five possible explanations for Emile's death from the arsenic found within his body:

1. *Emile accidentally poisoned himself.* It had been suggested as far back as Madeleine's arrest that Emile, in thinking he was taking some kind of medication, ingested the poison by mistake. The problem with this scenario is fourfold: Emile's noted dislike of taking medicine; his apparent health on the night of March 22 as witnessed by Mrs. Jenkins and Mary Tweedle; the lack of an arsenic container among his possessions; and the absence of his name in all Poison Books in the vicinity of Glasgow, Stirling, and the roads in between.

2. *Emile committed suicide, probably with the intent of framing Madeleine for his death.* This would explain not only the mysterious entries in his journal, but also his sudden decision to keep a diary for the last two months of his life. A suicide, however, would still leave some questions unanswered: Why did he journey all the way from Bridge of Allan to Glasgow on that final night, if all he intended to do was kill himself? And if his first two illnesses were unsuccessful attempts at self-destruction, why would he attempt it a third time, especially as the method was so painful and had failed twice—why did he not try some other method? Another puzzle, as with the accidental poisoning scenario, is how he obtained the arsenic without leaving a record. Most importantly, for this scenario to be plausible, Emile would need to know that Madeleine had recently been purchasing arsenic, and how could he have known that?

3. *Someone other than Madeleine murdered Emile, purposely or inadvertently implicating Madeleine in his death.* Madeleine's defense team never brought forth another person who might have wanted Emile dead, and no subsequent studies of the case have ever revealed such a person. While people's opinions of Emile varied, not even his detractors apparently disliked him enough that they would want to end his life. Additionally, for a person to kill Emile with the intent of framing Madeleine, he or she would need to possess two distinct pieces of information:

- Emile and Madeleine were involved in a romantic relationship, and
- Madeleine had recently made purchases of arsenic.

Emile's coworkers, Mary Perry, Monsieur de Mean, and Christina Haggart knew of the illicit love affair; and the various apothecaries and Mary Ann Buchanan knew of the arsenic purchases (with the possible addition of the mysterious "young lady" who George Carruthers Haliburton testified accompanied Madeleine during her second purchase)—but nobody knew of both, except Madeleine. If this were a typical "love triangle," William Minnoch would be the most likely suspect—but Minnoch did not know Emile personally and only learned of Madeleine's arsenic purchases and of Madeleine's relationship with Emile after Emile's death.

4. *Emile was killed by someone who did not know of his relationship with Madeleine, and/or did not even know Madeleine existed.* For Emile to have come across a murderous stranger or acquaintance on that fatal night, and for that person to choose, of all possible murder weapons, the specific poison that Emile's lover had recently been purchasing, relies on too many stark coincidences to be seriously considered.

5. *Madeleine killed Emile.* The circumstantial evidence makes a strong case against her. Her sudden interest in arsenic, combined with her upcoming mar-

riage to Minnoch, her hasty flight to Rowaleyn, and her lie about Emile's presence in the Blythswood Square house certainly arouse suspicions.

On the other hand, the blatant openness of her arsenic purchases and her lack of a single attempt to retrieve her incriminating letters after Emile's death show that if she did kill him, she was either unnaturally lucky or uncommonly naive, as she made significant errors at every turn: She knew that Christina Haggart could testify about Emile's visits inside the Blythswood Square home; she made no attempt to disguise her arsenic purchases, even bringing her own eyewitness with her to one (or two) of those purchases; and, unless Emile had told her differently, she knew that all of her letters were still among Emile's possessions—and she was fully aware of their potential for destroying her if they were discovered.

What actually happened to Emile in the early hours of March 23, 1857, will never be known. But one curious fact is inevitable: as Emile lay there, dying from the ingestion of a massive quantity of arsenic, he must have at least suspected the presence of something toxic in the "dark liquid" that he had recently consumed. Both Mary Perry and her brother-in-law stated that in the weeks before his death Emile had mentioned the possibility of his being poisoned.

And if, on his deathbed, he once again suspected poison, then his thoughts would naturally turn toward how the substance was given to him—and by whom. His silence on this topic from 2:30 in the morning until his death almost nine hours later is probably the greatest puzzle of this perplexing story.

Part VII

After the Trial

WITHIN A WEEK of her acquittal, Madeleine wrote separate letters to the matron and the chaplain of the Edinburgh prison, giving the world its sole glimpse of Madeleine's life and state of mind after being in the harsh spotlight of what the newspapers had christened the "trial of the century."

DEAR MISS AITKEN.

You shall be glad to hear I am well—in fact, I am quite well, and my spirits not in the least down. I left Edinburgh and went to Slateford, and got home to Rowaleyn during the night. But, alas, I found Mama in a bad state of health. But I trust in a short time all will be well with her. The others are all well. The feeling in the west is not so good towards me as you kind Edinburgh people showed me. I rather think it shall be necessary for me to leave Scotland for a few months, but Mama is so unwell we do not like to fix anything at present.

If you ever see Mr. C. Combe [the foreman of the jury], tell him that I, the panel, was not at all pleased with the verdict, [although] I was delighted with the loud cheer the court gave. I did not feel in the least put about when the jury were out considering whether they should send me home or keep me.

I think I must have had several hundred letters, all from gentlemen, some offering me consolation, and some their hearths and homes. My "friend" I know nothing of. I have not seen him. I hear he has been ill, which I don't much care.

I hope you will give me a note. Thank Miss Bell and Agnes in my name for all their kindness and attention to me. I should like you to send me my Bible and watch to [my father's office at] 124 St. Vincent Street, Glasgow. The country is looking most lovely. As soon as I know my arrangements I shall let you know where I am to be sent to. With kind love to yourself and Mr. Smith, ever believe me, yours sincerely,

MADELEINE SMITH.

July 15, 1857

DEAR MR. ROSE,

After the kind interest you showed me, I think it is but fair I should let you know of my safe arrival home. I am very well, and my spirits are good.

I found Mama far, far from well, but I trust she will soon be convalescent.

The feeling here is, I gather, strong against me, so I rather think I shall have to leave Scotland for a few weeks, but the poor state of Mama's health renders it impossible for me to make arrangements at present.

I was not at all pleased with the "verdict," but I was charmed with the loud cheer the court gave me. I got out of Edinburgh in the most private manner possible.

I trust that painful, unhappy affair may tend to do us all great good—I see a different feeling pervades our family circle already. I am so glad they all view it as an affliction sent from God for past errors and crimes, and if this be the means of drawing a family to the feet of Christ, I shall not grumble at the pain that sad event cost me. I may live to hear my family exclaim that it was the most blessed day of their life—the day I was cast into prison. God grant it may be so. I shall ever remember your kindness to me. Receive my deepest, warmest, and heartfelt thanks and, with kind regards, believe me, yours sincerely,

MADELEINE SMITH.

William Minnoch is harshly dismissed in Miss Aitken's letter as an ill "friend" that Madeleine no longer cares about. His engagement with Madeleine severed, he later married another and became a successful businessman and a leader of the Glasgow Chamber of Commerce.

The public's interest in the case did not die down after the trial's conclusion. Various newspapers continued to print articles about the trial, the verdict, and anything that was even remotely related to the case. The *Glasgow Herald* ran a story claiming that a man had gone to the Crown authorities and stated that between midnight and one o'clock in the morning on March 23, he saw a man and woman in the lane behind the Smith house. The witness verified that the man looked like Emile, and the woman was not "an ordinary street walker." Unfortunately, the *Herald* reported, the gentleman went to the authorities too late to qualify as a witness for the trial.

The major newspapers all printed summaries of the trial soon after Madeleine's release, and their opinions on the guilt of Madeleine and on the integrity of the two principal individuals varied widely.

The *Times* said: "The jury by their verdict have declared their inability to decide. In this verdict we must concur, yet we see no reason for the cheering and the manifestation of joy which greeted it. . . . Madeleine Smith goes free from the penalties of the law—and that is all."

In the *Spectator*: "The correspondence tends to show that L'Angelier led on his companion in guilt. Many remarks indicate that even the nauseous and sickly expressions of studied fondness in her letters were dictated by his reproaches of 'coldness'; and it is clear that he exercised an influence of the most baneful kind. . . . Her own character cannot be positively settled unless we go beyond the jury and confirm or reject the charge against her. Is she a Lucretia Borgia or is she only a boarding school miss, led by a designing and theatrical Frenchman into a copy of Parisian romance?"

The *Saturday Review*: "She found that she had ventured everything on an unworthy object, and the very depth of her love was changed, [by] the complete and perfect sense of utter loss, into the corresponding depth of hatred. . . ."

The *Glasgow Sentinel*: "[Madeleine Smith was] as much the seducer as the seduced. And when once the veil of modesty was thrown aside, from the first a very frail and flimsy one, the woman of strong passion and libidinous tendencies at once reveals herself. . . . [Madeleine is] one of those abnormal spirits that now and then rise up in society to startle and appall us. . . ."

The *Glasgow Citizen*: "In her first efforts at retrieval [of her letters], she found herself not in the arms of a protector but in the coils of a reptile."

The *Scotsman*: "[Madeleine Smith is] either the most fortunate of criminals or the most unfortunate of women."

The *Perthshire Courier*: "Of L'Angelier it were idle to speak. The wretch is dead."

The *Examiner*: ". . . to Madeleine Smith alone his horrible death seems to have been no shock, no grief, and she demeaned herself [at] her trial as if L'Angelier had never had a place in her affections. If it had been a trial for poisoning a dog the indifference could not have been greater."

In addition to the countless newspaper and magazine articles generated by the trial, noteworthy authors of the day also shared their opinions of the case. George Eliot wrote scathingly to her publisher that she felt Madeleine was the most unexciting of all murderesses and that Madeleine would no doubt find more victims for her nefarious research into cosmetics.

Folklorist Andrew Lang was thirteen years old when the initial newspaper headlines reported the arrest of an unnamed Glasgow woman for murder. Lang playfully told his friends that the lady in question must be the sister of his schoolmate, James Smith. To his shock, Lang soon discovered that he was entirely correct.

Several years after the trial, Henry James wrote that he was surprised the description of Emile's painful final hours did not lead to a guilty verdict, and he mourned the fact that no photograph of the young Madeleine had survived.

The ambrotype portraits of Emile and Madeleine, which had been present throughout the trial, vanished soon after—the souvenirs of a court attendant, perhaps. They resurfaced almost 130 years later in a bookseller's catalog, and were purchased by the Mitchell Library in Glasgow, which already possessed a collection of Madeleine's letters and various memorabilia from the trial.

Another keepsake from the trial, the original of a famous sketch depicting the full courtroom during the trial, was purchased from the artist by Charles T. Combe, the foreman of Madeleine's jury. The drawing had originally appeared in an 1857 newspaper and would later be used in several of Madeleine's biographies.

Emile's mother, reportedly overcome with grief at the death of yet another of her children, had Emile's name added to the family tombstone in Jersey. His body would stay in Glasgow, however, as the Langelier family could not afford to have his remains shipped back to Jersey, despite his mother's pleas and an unsuccessful campaign in Scotland to raise the necessary funds.

The Smith family continued to distance themselves from the notoriety of the case, keeping up appearances, but moving away from Glasgow: first to Bridge of Allan and then to Polmont by the Stirling-Edinburgh Road. On the surface, their neighbors were cordial, but the family would forever be the topic of whispered conversations and curious stares as they walked down the street. The family's days of attending balls and cultural events were over.

Madeleine's family members were not the only ones to find the trial's legacy inescapable. John Inglis built a strong reputation on his handling of the defense's case and quickly rose up the ranks of the Scottish legal system. He later became Lord Justice General, Lord President of the Court of Session, an author of several respected legal books, and a senior official of Glasgow, St. Andrews, and Edinburgh universities. A story still circulates of him: he was once asked at a dinner party if he truly believed that Madeleine was innocent of the murder charge. After a thoughtful pause, he said simply that he would "rather have danced than supped with her."

In the years after her trial, gossip ran rampant about Madeleine secretly leaving Scotland and going to Canada or Australia. One rumor, stating that Madeleine had married a surgeon named Tudor Hora and moved to Australia, persisted for decades despite an accumulation of facts proving it to be incorrect.

In reality, not long after her trial, Madeleine moved with her brother, Jack, to London and lived in a flat on Sloane Street. There she met George Wardle, a draftsman and the business manager of the artist William Morris. George and Madeleine were married in St. Paul's Church in Knightsbridge on July 4, 1861. Madeleine's father, either to keep up appearances or possibly out of mere relief, attended the wedding and gave the couple a substantial monetary gift.

George and Madeleine lived in a small house at 9 Charlotte Street in the London parish of St. George's Bloomsbury. Madeleine hosted many parties for her husband's artist friends, and they encouraged her to finally take up the art of watercolors. Madeleine is also credited with some of the needlework in Morris's textile projects.

Over time, the Wardles became involved in the Socialism movement, and Madeleine apparently acted either as the treasurer for a Socialist group or merely oversaw meetings and refreshments in the Wardle home. George Bernard Shaw went to a few of the meetings and described her as "an ordinary, good-humored, capable woman with nothing sinister about her."

Madeleine's father died in 1863. Her mother and Bessie died soon afterwards. Jack continued to live in England, while James and Janet remained in Scotland.

The Blythswood Square home was sold not long after Madeleine's trial. The building would later house the British Legal Life Assurance Company, an art school, and, during the last quarter of the twentieth century, the offices of a legal firm.

The complete Wardle family appears in the 1881 Census Index for London under the heading *London, St. George's*:

George Y. WARDLE, 45, Head, Artist (Painter), b. Leek, Staffordshire

Madeleine WARDLE, 44, Wife, b. Scotland

Mary WARDLE, 18, Daughter, b. Middlesex, London

Thomas WARDLE, 17, Son, Southwold, Suffolk

Mary BOBYER, 24, Servant

After twenty-eight years of marriage, and apparently in response to general marital discord, George resigned from William Morris & Company in 1889 and journeyed off to reside alone in Italy.

That same year, Madeleine once again became the focus of legal proceedings, albeit inadvertently. A man named Malcolm NacLeod Nicholson sold a stack of documents to a Glasgow bookseller, claiming that they were originals of some of Madeleine's letters to Emile. The bookseller doubted their authenticity, but purchased them anyway. Several weeks later, a gentleman browsing in the bookshop showed an interest in the letters. This man was a Clerk of the Peace in Glasgow, and he recognized his own handwriting in the marginal notations of some of the letters. Asking the bookseller how he came to own the documents, the Clerk reported the situation to the proper officials and Nicholson, a former clerk in Edinburgh's Justiciary Office, went on trial and was sentenced to one year in prison, as the letters were still the legal property of the government.

After George Wardle moved to Italy, Madeleine remained in London, eventually moving to Leek, where she supposedly lived on a vast estate owned by George's brother. From there she made a rare journey to Scotland to visit her sister, Janet, in Falkirk, using the name of Mrs. Lena Wardle—*Lena* being a childhood nickname Bessie had given her. After George's death from cancer in 1910, she reportedly emigrated to America (where her son, Thomas, had already emigrated to attend college) and eventually married a younger man named Sheehy.

With her new husband and new life, Mrs. Lena Wardle Sheehy once again endeavored to live a life of anonymity in New York City, although her infamous past followed close at her heels. Wild rumors of her living (or dying) in places such as Australia and France appeared from time to time in various newspapers, and these articles occasionally featured "direct interviews." As Madeleine actively avoided public attention, however, chances are she refused to grant such interviews, so it is hard to discern which, if any, of Madeleine's "quotes" are genuine. These stories reported her either living in miserable poverty or else owning the "cottage" she lived in as well as several other properties.

One article that appeared in an April 1927 edition of the *New York Sunday Chronicle* had several lengthy quotes from her, but erroneously reported that she lived in the central United States and continually paid for Catholic Masses to be said for Emile's soul. Lena Sheehy was still living in New York in 1927—and it would be extremely unlikely that Madeleine had ever arranged Masses for Emile, not only because she clearly wanted to leave her past behind her, but also because Emile, at his death, was a Protestant who was buried in a Protestant churchyard.

It was also reported that a Hollywood movie studio once asked Madeleine to be involved in a film based on her famous trial. She refused. The movie studio then threatened to go to the United States government and have her sent back to Scotland as an "undesirable alien" who was living off government welfare.

After Madeleine proved both her self-sufficiency and her legal marriage to Sheehy, an American, the deportation threats were dropped.

If, as writer Nigel Morland has stated, Madeleine's second husband is buried in St. Raymond's Cemetery in New York, then he is undoubtedly the *William A. Sheehy* who died of carcinoma of the esophagus on July 28, 1926, at St. Luke's Hospital. According to his death certificate, Mr. Sheehy was sixty-four years old, a "checker" by trade, and lived on Eighth Avenue in New York City.

Lena Wardle Sheehy passed away two years later, on April 12, 1928, dying of uremia poisoning, a form of kidney disease. Her address, at death, was listed as 4298 Park Avenue, New York City.

A few days after her death, Violet Carren, possibly a relative, purchased the burial plot at Mount Hope Cemetery in Hastings-on-Hudson, New York, that would become Mrs. Sheehy's final resting place.

Part VIII

What the Writers Said

THE TRIAL OF MADELEINE Hamilton Smith would live on in the public consciousness long after she had left the courtroom, although the trial's legacy would not be a legal one.

Clare Connelly, a Lecturer in Criminal Law at the University of Glasgow School of Law, believes "the legal importance of this case may not be in the evidence which was presented or the procedure adopted—which did not significantly affect the development of Scottish Criminal Law. Rather, a more probable reason why this case has attracted widespread interest is because of the sensationalist affair Miss Smith was alleged to have been having with the deceased and also the fact that women did not then and still rarely do commit homicide. An important aspect of the case may be the effect of the woman's gender on the outcome of the case. Inglis's address to the jury played on the fact that the accused is a respectable female and that the consequence of a guilty plea would be death. This may be one of the earliest reported cases where a chivalrous plea to the male jury may have affected the outcome of the case."

If her legacy was not a legal one, Madeleine Smith certainly became firmly established as a social celebrity. Later biographers and journalists would paint Madeleine in a spectrum of roles: a cold-blooded murderess, an innocent victim of the rigid role of Victorian women, or a selfish and thoughtless elitist. Emile, in turn, would be portrayed as everything from a poor, naive immigrant to a malicious brute who deserved to die.

Madeleine was scarcely out of the courthouse before publishers began printing books to feed the minds of the curious public. Transcripts of the trial, including fuller texts of the scandalous letters, began appearing as early as the autumn of 1857.

In 1864, the author Emma Robinson produced a three-volume novel about the case, entitled *Madeleine Graham*, and more than a century later, Glen Petrie's novel, *Mariamne*, and Pamela Elizabeth West's book, *Madeleine*, would similarly fictionalize Madeleine's story.

Plays such as Winifred Duke's *Madeleine Smith: A Tragi-Comedy*, Howard M. Lockhart's *The Story of Madeleine Smith*, and *The Rest Is Silence* brought Madeleine's story to the stage—and a musical based on Madeleine's life is reportedly in preparation in Great Britain as of this writing.

The movie that inspired the deportation threats was never made, assuming that the film in question was not entirely the product of a reporter's fanciful imagination. Two other early movies, however, are supposedly inspired by Madeleine's story: *Letty Lynton* (1932), in which Joan Crawford's character poisons an unwanted suitor named "Emile Renaul," and *Dishonored Lady* (1947), in which Madeleine Damien (Hedy Lamarr) murders a rejected lover.

It wasn't until 1949, when David Lean's film, *Madeleine*, premiered, that a movie based on the actual events appeared. The film was riddled with problems, however, the largest being that the movie never took a stand as to whether Madeleine killed Emile or not, leaving it open-ended and vague. Also, at the age of forty, Lean's wife, Ann Todd, was far too old to play the twenty-year-old Madeleine, but Todd had played Madeleine in a London stage production of *The Rest Is Silence* and wanted to portray her on the big screen. The film remains one of Lean's few cinematic failures.

The first nonfiction books devoted to the case were merely reproductions of the trial transcripts. Writers and criminologists would later analyze the case in greater detail, however, and come to varying conclusions as to the particulars of the case and of the two principals involved.

Joseph Forster devoted a brief chapter to Madeleine's story in his 1896 book about famous crimes, *Studies in Black and Red*. Forster gave a cursory recitation of the facts, but did not mention significant items, such as Emile's notebook or Madeleine's flight to Row. Edited versions of four letters were included, but Forster warned that many of Madeleine's letters "assume an erotic fervour that forbids quotation."

In 1905, A. Duncan Smith (apparently no relation to Madeleine) combined the letters and trial transcripts into a book, entitled *The Trial of Madeleine Smith*. In his introduction, Smith stated that no criminal trial before Madeleine's had seen the possibilities of guilt and innocence so "evenly balanced," and it was only the prosecution's inability to prove that the couple had met previous to any of Emile's illnesses that caused the jury to decide how they did. Smith also placed much credit for the verdict on one unnamed jury member, who had a "masterful dominance" over the others. This man's "sympathies for the accused were as active as was his resolution to do all he could in her behalf."

Smith went on to theorize that Christina Haggart had not been entirely truthful in her testimony, and the housemaid knew more than she had revealed in court.

As an appendix to his book, Smith included an undated phrenological analysis of the bumps on Madeleine's head:

> This young lady's head is of an English form, and of the usual size, but more than usual force of character, owing to large combativeness, self-esteem, love of approbation, and firmness, powerful affections. She possesses both the masculine and feminine qualities, more especially the former. Has great talent for engineering, architecture, designing, and surveying; should be very good at mathematics. The drawbacks to these talents is a warm, sanguine temperament, great love of traveling, varied scenery, variety of study. Requires amusement and recreation. A great flirt; will at all times have a warm side towards gentlemen, and will prefer their society to that of her own sex. They will be fond of her, for she possesses a magnetism which will draw them round her like bees round a rose tree. Owing to her strong affections and healthy temperament, she will make a treasure of a wife to a worthy husband. Kind to animals; fond of horses, dogs, etc. Just and generous. Fiery, quick temper, her anger not lasting. Not large in veneration. Has a chance to be religious. Great love for the fine arts. Martial music will please her. Memory good for events, faces, places, and history. Will enjoy a little fun and drollery and conviviality. Orderly, and has great taste for dress. Reasoning powers good. Apt to look on the bright side of things. On the whole, a very clever head.

The writer F. Tennyson Jesse addressed the case in her 1927 book, *Trial of Madeleine Smith*. Clearly pro-Madeleine, Jesse spoke of Madeleine's "invincible spirit" and "hard brightness," and admired the "excellent state of her nervous system." Emile, however, is reduced to "that little, scheming, sensual, iron-willed lady-killer," and a practitioner of "such devious ways." Jesse stated that she, along with most students of the case, believe that Madeleine did murder Emile—but he deserved it.

Jesse took no stance as to the authenticity of Emile's diary notebook, but stated that she found Emile's deathbed silence regarding how he had received the fatal dose to be the most puzzling aspect of the entire story.

Madeleine, Jesse felt, was really a woman born too soon, who came along at "a period of the world's history which was the most hopeless for a nature such as hers." She would have been better suited to the early twentieth century, Jesse postulated, where she could have enjoyed a life in business, the theater, or driving ambulances during World War I. Such diversions would have been a better outlet and she would not have had to stoop to "scheming and deception."

Geoffrey L. Butler's 1935 *Madeleine Smith* reexamined the case, and he painted the love affair darkly: Madeleine's "perverted streak" liked it when Emile reproved her, and a "masochistic tendency" caused her to relish that treatment with a "morbid pleasure" and to "glory in his harshness." Emile, for his part, was not the naive man some claim him to be: he was "sufficiently practiced in such love-making" and practiced "skillful wooing." Emile's "main object [was that] of a wealthy marriage," and he "clearly had no desire to be saddled with a disinherited daughter."

Butler theorized that Madeleine used a false name to purchase arsenic before Emile's first illness, and, seeing how easy it was to obtain the poison, made her subsequent three purchases outright.

Butler was the first to conclude that Lena Wardle Sheehy and Madeleine Smith were the same person, and he presented two interesting glimpses of her later life, either of which may or may not be true. First, he credited Madeleine, during her years married to George Wardle (whom Butler does not name, for discretionary purposes) as the initiator of the custom of removing the tablecloth from the table at mealtimes and setting placemats directly onto the wood surface. How shocking that would be to the late Victorian mind can only be guessed. Secondly, Butler curiously assigned Madeleine's life in America as taking place in New Orleans, where he also maintained that her husband died. Butler unfortunately gave no citation for this notion of Madeleine's life in Louisiana, and William Sheehy clearly died in New York City, leading to the belief that Butler was mistaken or misled.

Butler also put forth a theory regarding Emile's deathbed silence that had puzzled Jesse, saying that Emile's reticence proves that Madeleine had murdered him. If anyone else had given him the poison, Butler reasoned, Emile would have said something to Mrs. Jenkins or Dr. Steven to ensure that his beloved Madeleine would not be implicated.

William Roughead addressed the case in an essay that appeared in his 1937 collection, *Mainly Murder*. Although the title of the piece proclaims Madeleine "a Wonder Heroine of the 'Fifties," Roughead quickly categorizes her as "false, self-centered, wholly regardless of the rights and feelings of others . . . and her treatment of her blameless suitor, Mr. Minnoch, was flagrantly perfidious." He disagreed with Jesse's statement that had Madeleine lived in later years she would have turned out differently: "[in] this golden age of lipstick, cocktails, and nightclubs, she would infallibly have gone wrong." Roughead said that viewing the drawings of Madeleine at the trial shows "a horse-faced female of repellent aspect," and Emile is depicted: "he has been called blackguard and blackmailer . . . [but] it was neither revenge nor money that he wanted, but his wife."

The principal characters so summarized, Roughead then gave a brief accounting of the evidence. He believed Emile's diary to be authentic, and stated that its suppression from the jury was responsible for the eventual outcome of the trial. He maintained, as later writers would, that Scots law in the mid-1800s might have legally considered Emile and Madeleine to *be* married, due to their sexual relations and the fact that they addressed each other as "husband" and "wife" in their correspondence.

During the 1940s, the poet Sacheverell Sitwell's book, *Splendours and Miseries*, attempted a more literary slant to the tale. To achieve this, Sitwell drew a different Emile than had previously been seen: "[he] is frightened of her. She is so strong in character." Emile was taken along by her desires, which he complied with agreeably, but he was weak at heart. Sitwell waxed overly poetic in his treatment, spending nine pages depicting Emile's wait near Rowaleyn on the night of their first sexual encounter, and an entire page describing arsenic-eating Styrian peasants.

Sitwell put forth that both Emile and Madeleine were active arsenic eaters, and Emile could easily have obtained his own supply when he was in Paris during the Revolution—a small amount, Sitwell assured us, would have lasted for several years. Why Emile's Parisian arsenic was not then found among his possessions after his death is not addressed.

Unfortunately, Sitwell showed a lack of knowledge concerning specific facts of the case. He stated that Madeleine's sisters were brought up in total ignorance of the shameful saga concerning their eldest sister. This is not possible, as Janet testified at the trial and Bessie was present at Emile's introduction to Madeleine and had actually passed notes between the two. Sitwell's scenario of Emile's final night is equally spurious: Emile took the cup, fully knowing what was in it, but his love for Madeleine was so great that he played dumb and drank the fatal cocoa. His deathbed summons for Miss Perry was merely to tell his friend that he had forgiven his beloved Madeleine. It is hard to believe this kind of self-sacrificing behavior would come from the same man who had forbidden Madeleine to walk on public streets with her siblings or speak politely to guests at parties, and had pointed out her "very bad faults" from the start of their relationship.

One speculative bit of trivia that Sitwell alone stated: during Madeleine's years among the William Morris artistic circle, the painter Rosetti used her as a model for several paintings he created of Mary Magdelene.

In the 1950s, Madeleine's life and trial was addressed again in three books: Nigel Morland's *That Nice Miss Smith*, Peter Hunt's *The Madeleine Smith Affair*, and Edgar Lustgarten's *The Woman in the Case*.

Morland drew clear-cut pictures of the two principals: Emile was completely false and Morland believed nothing he ever said. He was charming only to get his own way, and was ruled by jealousy. Madeleine, in comparison, was strong-willed and afraid of nothing—except her father. She never sincerely meant to marry Emile, but merely paid him "lip service." Madeleine's actions were simply her rebellions at the stifling life of a young woman in that society. Morland claimed that both were matched in their ability to manipulate the other, but that Madeleine was ultimately in control of the relationship. This delicate balance went awry when Emile threatened to show her letters to her father, which Morland claimed was not a real attempt at blackmail, just Emile's attempt to frighten her. It worked, but also succeeded in infuriating Madeleine, who was like a "child playing recklessly with fire, to be outraged and frightened when it proved hot."

Morland believed Emile's diary to be genuine, although he didn't particularly elaborate on its significance. He also believed that Emile was the man who accompanied the auctioneer, Ross, on that long walk from Coatbridge to Glasgow, but did not address that same man's puzzling references to the town of Alloa.

Peter Hunt's treatment presented no new theories, although it did introduce some letters that had never been previously published. The book begins with a short foreword by Roughead, and points back, in some ways, to Butler's sado-masochistic theories, with Hunt seeing "again and again the letters are punctuated with Madeleine's desire, indeed determination, to be dominated."

Hunt saw Emile as "weak, not wicked; sensuous without breeding; bigoted, not merely revengeful, in no way a match for a girl he fondly imagined would be content to identify herself with him and his." Indeed, Emile was "out of his depth with her" and she enjoyed his tyranny "so long as she was in love with him." Hunt pointed out that many of the witnesses painted a picture of Emile as warm and friendly, and only with Madeleine did he become demanding and relentless.

Madeleine, Hunt felt, "was intelligent . . . [and] had fate dealt the cards in another order [she might have taken] her place . . . beside the greatest women of the 19th century."

Crime writer Lustgarten's *The Woman in the Case*, a collection recalling four famous murder trials involving women, devoted one section to Madeleine. Lustgarten was neutral regarding her character, but classified Emile bluntly: "a hypocritical prig . . . a born blackmailer, and of a type more contemptible than most . . . a mean and cunning opportunist with an undeviating eye of personal advantage, he planned . . . to entrap this . . . well-placed girl [so she] would have no choice but to become his wife."

Lustgarten concluded his chapter with a flight of fancy: an imaginary transcript of Madeleine's testimony had she actually taken the stand—a situation that would not have been possible until the 1898 Act of Parliament which allowed prisoners to speak in court in their own defense.

In the 1970s, Richard Altick and Mary S. Hartman both devoted chapters to Madeleine in their books about infamous Victorian murders. Altick's *Victorian Studies in Scarlet* presented Madeleine as a "determined and resourceful young lady," and stated that anti-French feelings in Scotland at the time of the trial contributed as much to the verdict as did the prosecution's failure to present a strong case.

Hartman's *Victorian Murderesses* painted a dark portrait of Madeleine. In Hartman's view, Madeleine initiated the first sexual encounter and continually used Emile's lower social status as a justification for her insensitive behavior toward him.

Additionally, Hartman proposed new theories that do not seem to be based on actual evidence, and actually contradict Madeleine's letters and the trial testimony in several places. Hartman believed that the family confrontations reported in Madeleine's letters were fabrications, and no one in Madeleine's family actually knew of her continuing relationship with Emile. While Madeleine had confessed in her pleading letter of February 9, 1857, that: "[Madeleine's mother] did not boast of anything I had said of you—for she, poor woman, thought I had broken off with you last winter," there is no reason to believe that the earlier conflicts with Madeleine's parents (or, for that matter, *any* of the incidents involving Madeleine's siblings) were not genuine.

Additionally, Hartman presented the hypothesis that Madeleine blackmailed Christina Haggart into helping her, holding her knowledge of the illicit visits from Christina's fiancé, Duncan MacKenzie, over the housemaid until she would act as an accomplice. Nothing in the letters or trial testimony, however, show that MacKenzie's visits were anything but common knowledge within the Smith household. At the conclusion of her testimony, the Lord Justice Clerk had remarked to Christina, "I suppose . . . as MacKenzie was coming to visit you, you were anxious to oblige the young lady." But this statement most likely implies that Christina wanted to remain in Madeleine's good graces so that Madeleine would not put a stop to MacKenzie's routine visits—but does not necessarily imply that those visits were unknown to the Smith family.

All of Madeleine's biographers, detractors and defenders alike, have agreed on one issue: when she wrote in one of her later letters to Emile, "I put on paper what I should not," she spoke with stark and all-encompassing truth. Had Emile not stockpiled her letters, or had Madeleine and Emile's affair been limited exclusively to clandestine meetings, there would almost certainly have been a different outcome to their ill-fated love affair.

Part IX

A Brief and Final Puzzle

WRITERS FROM GEOFFREY L. BUTLER forward have unanimously believed that when Lena Wardle Sheehy died at three o'clock in the morning on April 12, 1928, she took all of Madeleine Smith's secrets with her.

Mrs. Sheehy's official death certificate, however, presents two problems. First, her age on the document is listed as sixty-four, which would make 1864 the year of her birth, a full seven years after Emile's death in 1857. Madeleine Smith would have been ninety-three in 1928. While it might be possible for an overworked morgue doctor to hurriedly sign a death certificate and make such a mistake, the death certificate clearly states that the same physician who signed that certificate had "attended the deceased from March 13, 1928 to April 11, 1928." It requires a great deal of belief in an ill and elderly woman's youthful appearance and/or a doctor's gullibility and ineptitude to believe that a medical professional, who had cared for a patient while she was living, would think she was almost thirty years younger than she actually was.

Another problem on the certificate is when it states the number of years the deceased had been "in U.S. (if of foreign birth)" as "about 36 years." This would place Mrs. Sheehy's immigration into the United States in the early 1890s. All of the scholars of Madeleine Smith's case, however, claim that Madeleine emigrated from England only *after* George Wardle's death in 1910.

Granted, we do not know the source of the death certificate's information: the doctor could have obtained it from the patient herself, or possibly from an acquaintance of the deceased. And, admittedly, Madeleine had spent most of her adult life evading her past, and she may have instructed others to give misleading information in order to keep the inquisitive off her trail. But twenty-nine years of an elderly woman's age is a remarkable amount to slip through a professional physician's fingers.

The doubt that Madeleine Smith and Lena Wardle Sheehy were the same person even spreads to the prestigious Online Computer Library Center, Inc. (OCLC), an organization that maintains the highest quality of library card-catalog information. A cross-section of the OCLC bibliographic records for Madeleine Smith show both 1893 and 1928 as the year of her death, and OCLC also includes an entry for "Hora, Madeleine Hamilton Smith," reflecting her marriage to the surgeon she never actually married.

Madeleine Smith and Lena Wardle Sheehy may indeed have been one and the same person. But like every other aspect of Madeleine's tale, there is ample room for doubt.

Bibliography

A variety of sources were consulted in preparing this book. The contemporary reports appearing in the *London Times* were especially useful in obtaining a clear picture of the trial and how it was perceived by a curious public. Of the numerous books on the subject, Peter Hunt's *The Madeleine Smith Affair* was the most helpful, featuring articles from other 1857 newspapers and several letters that had never appeared in Madeleine's previous biographies. Kevin Brownlow's book, *David Lean: A Biography*, provided detailed information on the three films inspired by Madeleine's life.

Altick, Richard D. *Victorian Studies in Scarlet*. New York: Norton, 1970.

Anonymous. *Trial of Miss Madeleine H. Smith, before the High Court of Justiciary, Edinburgh, June 30th to July 9th, 1857, for the Alleged Poisoning of M. Pierre Emile L'Angelier, at Glasgow : Special Verbatim Report, with Portraits and Plans*. Edinburgh: D. Mathers, 1857.

Bronlow, Kevin. *David Lean: A Biography*. New York: St. Martin's, 1996.

Butler, Geoffrey L. *Madeleine Smith*. London: Duckworth, 1935.

Forster, Joseph. *Studies in Black and Red*. London: Ward & Downey, 1896.

Hartman, Mary S. *Victorian Murderesses: A True History of Thirteen Respectable French and English Women Accused of Unspeakable Crimes*. New York: Schocken Books, 1976.

Hunt, Peter. *The Madeleine Smith Affair*. London: Carroll & Nicholson, 1950.

Jesse, F. Tennyson. *Trial of Madeleine Smith*. Edinburgh and London: W. Hodge & Company Ltd., 1927.

Lustgarten, Edgar. *The Woman in the Case*. New York: Charles Scribner's Sons, 1955.

Morison, John, ed. *A Complete Report of the Trial of Miss Madeleine Smith, for the Alleged Poisoning of Pierre Emile L'Angelier.* Edinburgh: William P. Nimmo, 1857.

Morland, Nigel. *That Nice Miss Smith.* London: F. Muller, 1957.

Roughead, William. *Mainly Murder.* London: Cassell and Company Ltd., 1937.

Sitwell, Sacheverell. *Splendours and Miseries.* London: Faber and Faber Ltd., 1943.

Smith, A. Duncan. *The Trial of Madeleine Smith.* Toronto: Canada Law Book Co., 1905.

Index

About the Author

DOUGLAS MACGOWAN is a freelance writer and author of numerous articles on Scottish issues in *Celtic Heritage*, *Scottish Journal*, and *The Highlander*.